THE ARMIES OF INDIA

Gardner's Horse, 1850

THE
ARMIES OF INDIA

PAINTED BY

MAJOR A. C. LOVETT

THE GLOUCESTERSHIRE REGIMENT

DESCRIBED BY

MAJOR G. F. MacMUNN, D.S.O.

ROYAL FIELD ARTILLERY

WITH FOREWORD BY

FIELD-MARSHAL EARL ROBERTS

V.C., K.G., K.P., O.M., Etc.

CRÉCY BOOKS

First published by A & C Black, 1911
Reprinted edition published by Crécy Books, 1984
Second printing, Crécy Books, 1988

Crécy Books, The Triangle
Somerton, Somerset TA11 6QJ

British Library Cataloguing in Publication Data

McMunn, *Sir* George
    The armies of India.
    1. Armies—India—History
    I. Title
    355.3'1'0954   UA847

    ISBN 0–947554–02–5

Printed and bound in Great Britain by
Biddles Ltd, Guildford and King's Lynn

CONTENTS

CHAPTER VI

CHAPTER VII

CHAPTER VIII

LIST OF ILLUSTRATIONS

Also nineteen smaller line drawings in the text.

FOREWORD

It will readily be believed that I have read this short history of the Armies of India, written by Major MacMunn and illustrated by Major Lovett, with the greatest interest. Having spent so many eventful years of my life in India, and having been so intimately associated with the Indian Army, in peace and war, I think that no one is better able than myself to esteem that Army at its proper value, as regards what it has—with the help of British training and example—achieved in the past, or to appreciate what it is capable of doing in the future under the same conditions. And this intimate knowledge of its capabilities enables me to realize to the fullest extent the enormous responsibility which rests upon all who are concerned with the administration and handling of such a splendid and potent machine. It is most imperfectly known in England, and often insufficiently understood in India, how diverse and divergent in many respects are the numerous races which we enlist into our Indian Army—in creed, in customs, in temperament, and traditions. Yet each and all of these factors must be attentively studied, and the most careful consideration given to the difference of treatment they impose in arranging the conditions of service for such widely different idiosyncrasies, if we would maintain and develop the fighting efficiency of our Indian soldiers, and the strength of the bonds of loyalty and devotion by which they are attached to our service. Major MacMunn's masterly review of the methods by which the existing army has attained its present state of perfection will greatly help to a proper understanding for the necessity of carefully studying the varying characteristics of the several Indian races; while the admirable illustrations by Major Lovett clearly depict the fine physical types we have in our Indian soldiers. For these reasons I cordially recommend this book to all who are interested in the welfare and prosperity of our great Indian Army — more particularly to all officers of the British and Indian Services whose duty must constantly bring them into contact with Indian troops.

In conclusion, let me say that no account of the Armies of India would be complete which did not include a description of the Imperial Service Troops organized and maintained by the Rulers of the great Feudatory States of Hindustan; and I am pleased, therefore, to see that the origin and development of these fine, serviceable troops are fully set forth in this volume. Encouraged by the British Government, and advised and assisted by British officers, these corps—personally led by their own Princes—have more than justified the high expectations formed of them when their organization was first proposed; and they constitute, at the present time, a moral and material accession of strength to the paramount power which can hardly be overrated.

The joint authors of this interesting volume have done their work well, and I hope that their interesting and instructive narrative will have the wide circulation which it deserves.

ROBERTS, F.M.

THE ARMIES OF INDIA

CHAPTER I

THE ARMY OF THE HONOURABLE EAST INDIA COMPANY

" By the legion's road to Rimini."

THE English have as yet ruled in India barely one-half the time that the Romans ruled in Britain, though their rule in the East has much in common with that of Rome north of the Channel. For the last century and a half have the English legions, European and Indian, tramped the trunk roads of Hindustan as those of Rome tramped Merry England before it was England at all. Up and down the length and breadth of India, as up and down Watling Street and the Via Fossa, or up and down "the legion's road to Rimini," at the legion's pace, have tramped those English legions since Clive decided that there should be one king and not a dozen in India, and that one, neither French nor Dutch nor Portuguese.

And the marvel of it all is that these tramping disciplined legions are not the beef and porridge and potato-reared lads of the Isles, but for the most part men of the ancient races of Hindustan, ruled and trained and led after the manner of the English.

From the doorkeepers and trained bands that first guarded the factories of the early merchants, the army of John Company *Bahadur* grew and prospered, by the secret of ever-increasing scope and labour, till it became the great shako-clad army of the Line that vanished for the most part in the tragedy of '57.

Of the three great presidential armies, the larger part, that of Bengal, and part of that of Bombay, disappeared, and with it the glorious record of successful war and faithful service, in a storm of unreasoned and uncalled-for mutiny, that buried in a month the tradition of a century.

The army that now upholds the Empire of Hindustan, is based on a systematic grouping of men by race and sept and clan, with a view to the full development of race efficiency.

This careful grouping has been the subject of much attention during the last twenty years, and has called for a thorough study of the clans and tribal systems of India, ending in a method of recruiting which is remarkable, and of a rank and file which is numerous and admirable. It is also well calculated to prevent the decline of martial qualities, which follows so quickly in the East on an era of peace. The results of twenty years of this system it is the object of this book to describe and illustrate. To arrive, however, at the present stage, and to understand that vast organization by class and clan which are illustrated herein, it is necessary to trace the rise of the armies of India through their separate presidential existence, to one vast whole.

It is proposed to deal with the subject in the following order :—

The Army of the Honourable East India Company.
The Army of the Great Mutiny.
The Armies as transferred to the Crown.
The Military clans and tribes.
The Indian Army of to-day.
The Armies of the Feudatory States.

The army of great John Company took its origin from three separate nuclei, separated by many miles of road and sea and hostile territory. These three centres originated in, first, "an ensign and thirty men," reinforced by a "gunner and his crew," stationed in Bengal towards the end of the seventeenth century; second, a detachment sent to garrison Bombay, the dower of Catherine of Braganza, Charles the Second's bride; and third, the forming of companies and soldiers from factory doorkeepers and watchmen in Madras. These curiously haphazard beginnings were the unmeditated foundations of three immense armies of horse, foot, and artillery.

The raising of actual native regiments was first undertaken by the French, and it was due to the coming struggle for mastery in Southern India that we owe the first conception of a regular native army. In 1748 Dupleix raised several battalions of Musalman soldiery armed in the European fashion in the Carnatic, and a few years later Stringer Lawrence followed suit in Madras. The distances that separated the three presidencies resulted in each force growing up on divergent principles and with different organizations, of which the ill results survive to some extent even to this day. European companies were formed from detachments sent from England, from runaway sailors, men of disbanded French corps, from Swiss and Hanoverians, from prisoners of war, and any white material in search of a livelihood. In 1748 the regular European corps of the Company's service, who now form part of the British Line and the Royal Artillery, were first formed from these heterogeneous detachments and scattered companies. In 1754 the first Royal troops came to take their share in garrisoning the East Indies, the 39th foot being the "first in the Indies." By 1759, two years after Plassey, six regular native battalions existed in Madras, and a few years later similar corps were formed in Bombay.

During the constant wars with the French, with Mysore and the Mahrattas, the presidential armies grew and developed and were brigaded. In 1793 the fall of Pondicherry for the last time ended once and for all the power of the French in India, though their influence lasted for many years after, and even in the year of grace 1911 there are old native officers to be found in the Feudatory States who can drill their men in French. When this great struggle came to an end, and Lord Cornwallis had humbled the Tiger of Mysore, and, after the manner of the English, given him one more chance, it became high time to put some organization and system into the mass of troops that had grown up during the years of war. So in 1795 we come upon the first general reconstruction, on a definite principle, throughout the three armies. At this date there were 13,000 Europeans in the country, King's and Company's, and some 24,000 native troops in Bengal and Madras respectively, with 9000 in Bombay. The reorganization took the accepted form of collecting artillery companies into battalions, cavalry troops into regiments, and forming the infantry into two-battalion regiments. This of course meant renumbering the whole of the battalions in each of the three armies except the first half, and incurring the usual dislike of corps for a change of the number under which they have won fame, however necessary that be. The uniforms of corps were more strictly assimilated to those of the King's troops, and a regular army came into being.

The result was as follows :—

Bengal.—European Artillery.　Three battalions of 5 companies each.
　European Infantry.　Three battalions of 10 companies each.
　Native Cavalry.　Four regiments.
　Native Infantry.　Twelve regiments of 2 battalions.

Madras—European Infantry. Two battalions of 10 companies.

      Artillery. Two European battalions of 5 companies each, with 15 companies of lascars.

      Native Cavalry. Four regiments.

      Native Infantry. Eleven regiments of 2 battalions.

Bombay.—European Artillery. Six companies.

      European Infantry. Two battalions of 10 companies.

      Native Infantry. Four regiments of 2 battalions and a marine battalion.

In those days the whole of India swarmed with men of military predilections. The Afghan races, who for the last sixty years have been cribbed and confined to their own hills, wandered at will through the land to sell their sword to the highest bidder. Every native chief had Arab and Afghan soldiery. Afghan soldiers of fortune, on the waning of the Mogul authority, had hacked their way to power and were forming principalities. The Rohillas, the descendants of Afghan and Turki settlers, still preserved many of their original characteristics, and drew fresh recruits from relatives in the border hills.

The old coast armies were largely filled by these adventurers or their half-bred children, or else by low-caste men, who on European food and with

European leading gladly fought the high‑caste races that had oppressed them. The irregular horse, which came into being in Lord Lake's time, was largely recruited from the soldiers of fortune and masterless men that broke away from the falling fortunes of the crumbling States. It should be remembered that in few cases were the rulers then going down before us more than mushroom kings—adventurers who had themselves displaced the old rulers or the old Mogul governors; in hardly any case had they more claim to power than "the good old rule; the simple plan." The slackening of the Mogul authority had been the signal for a vast scramble among the free‑lances, in which the cruelty and oppression endured by the long-suffering peasantry was beyond belief. To every district from which British successes had driven the free-lance and the alien *Schwartzreiter*, the British uniform and the white face were a sign of freedom and mercy, when the peasant dare till the field and the woman creep out from her hovel.

Then, too, because in every land, but more especially in the East, it is good to be on the winning side, soldiers of all kinds flocked to the Company's colours, and the leader of free-lances tried to preserve some *izzat* [1] in serving the new master, who at any rate paid regularly.

In 1798 Lord Mornington, later the Marquis Wellesley, " The great Marquis," became Governor-General, and, seeing farther ahead than most, realized that whatever the folk at home would say, the British in the East must either go forward or be overwhelmed, and that forthwith, and so determined that however so much others might care to fritter away an empire, he would have none of it. Already far-seeing men had settled that there was to be one European power in Hindustan, fighting the French wherever they found them, and Lord Mornington had determined that there should not only be one European power, but only one paramount power in the Peninsula. With the fall of the French State, French soldiers of fortune had drifted to most of the native courts of India, ready to minister to the desire for what then seemed the secret of power, troops trained on the European model. Mahratta and Musalman States, alarmed at the might of the English, were preparing to destroy the power of the Company. Buonaparte himself was openly trafficking with Tippoo in Mysore, with Scindia, with Holkar and the Bhonsla, the leading chiefs of the

---

[1] Prestige.

Mahratta confederacy, while the French Isles of France and Bourbon harboured privateers to prey on the Indiamen, and formed a base for designs on India itself.

So the great Marquis started forth himself to strike first, lest worse befall. Tippoo, the Tiger of Mysore, profiting little by the chance given him six years earlier by Lord Cornwallis, again broke a lance, and fell once and for all to General Harris. Arthur Wellesley and Stevenson broke the power of Scindia in two pitched battles and a dozen successful sieges and assaults. General Lake, the Commander-in-Chief, led his troops from Bengal against the chief gatherings of the Mahrattas, defeating Scindia's trained forces, the army that De Boigne and Perron had organized with such care, at Deig and Laswarrie. Delhi fell, the old blind Mogul was rescued from his Mahratta jailers and pensioned, and Holkar was chased by Lake for 350 miles, till he fled to his own country.

Then came the swing back of the pendulum, and the British took reverses that lessened their hold on the imagination of the East for many years to come. General Lake left the final pursuit of Holkar to a force under Colonel Monson of the 76th Foot, and that officer followed far away from his own base and into the season of the rains, till Holkar, tampering with his auxiliaries, and even with his regular troops, turned on him. Monson was compelled to retire, and the withdrawal gradually changed to a flight, and the flight to a debacle, despite the heroism of his Europeans, and some of his native troops. The second reverse was the Commander-in-Chief's failure to take Bhurtpore, the capital of a Hindu State. Time after time were his columns, usually headed by the 76th Foot, hurled back from the impracticable breaches with heavy loss, till at last the old soldier reluctantly determined to abandon the siege of the great mud fortress ; and for years after, when our action was thought high-handed, we were told to "go bully Bhurtpore." With the exception of these two failures, the three years' campaign against the Mahrattas was con- spicuous by its success, and by the treaties which brought the States concerned, not within the actual British Empire, but to a definite state of allied feudatories, with in many cases their power for evil at any rate much curtailed.

There is an old medal, so old that its youngest wearer has long passed to his rest, which com- memorates the days when the great sepoy army was evolving itself in the school of experience as an army of the Line, in battle and march and siege, earning much fame in the process. It bears the inscription, "To the Army of India," and its tally of clasps includes the history of the wars of the Marquis Wellesley, of Arthur Wellesley, his brother, and General Gerard Lake, the Commander-in-Chief, as well as the later victories of Lord Moira and Malcolm and Hislop. "Assaye," "Argaum," "Ghawilghur," "Asseerghur," "Laswarrie,' "Allighur," "Battle of Deig," "Capture of Deig," "Battle of Delhi," "Defence of Delhi," are among the honours that the medal commemorates, and which were borne on the colours of corps till, for the most part of the Bengal Army, they were wiped off the record in the whirlwind of Mutiny.

During these wars more regiments, both horse and foot, were continually being raised, and after them the army became still more regular and controlled by regulation, in close touch with the increasing garrison of King's troops, and more and more European in its dress and equipment. Irregulars too were added to the army at this period, and as the question of regulars versus irregulars has been hotly argued in India in the past, it may be well to understand the difference. To-day, the Silladar Cavalry are the legitimate heirs of the old irregulars, and the whole native army is largely modelled on what fifty years ago was termed the Irregular System. The regular army, both horse and foot, resembled in its organization the British Line. The establishment of officers resembled that of the King's service, and companies and troops were commanded by the British officers, while the native officers were but understudies promoted by seniority, and not for efficiency, and were men of great age. On the cross over the long trench graves on the battlefield of Chillianwalla are inscribed the names of two Brahman subadars, and against their names is recorded their ages, 65 and 70. In war time men no doubt came to commissioned rank earlier, but in peace under the regular system the native officers were aged figure-heads. In the irregular corps the British officers were few, and native officers had definite command of companies and troops, and came to great authority and efficiency thereby. The irregular cavalry were enlisted on the old system of the country—the sil-ladar system—whereby in return for a sum down the soldier came with horse, arms, and accoutrements complete. This is the system which, considerably developed, holds in the Indian cavalry to-day, with the exception of the three light cavalry regular regiments of the old Madras cavalry, which still exist as part of the old line, and which still wear the French grey and silver of the old regular light cavalry that played so leading a part in the Mutiny.

The irregulars were not esteemed at their worth by the rest of the army, till the wars in Afghanistan and the Punjab showed the immense value of the power of resource and initiative that they possessed. This was probably accentuated by the fact that while this spirit was far more present in all ranks in the earlier wars, the *Pax Britannica* had killed it among the peasantry and it only remained among a smaller class.

It should be remembered that during the earlier years of the nineteenth century the Indian army fulfilled an essentially imperial rôle. The reduction of the oversea colonies and naval stations of our European enemies during the Napoleonic wars was entrusted to it. The oversea expeditions were numerous, and this power to commence expeditions from a self-supporting base, was and is one of the great strategical assets which India adds to our imperial power.

So early as 1762, an expedition composed of Madras troops took part in the war with Spain by capturing Manila.

In 1795, an expedition from India captured
Ceylon from the Dutch and French, the native
troops being from Madras, with the exception of
some artillery companies from
Bengal.

In 1795, an expedition from
Madras captured Amboyna and
the Spice Islands from the Dutch.

In 1801, a force from India
under Sir David Baird proceeded
to join the British force in Egypt,
the 2nd and 13th Bombay Infantry and some native artillery
taking part.

In 1808, a force of volunteers
from the Bengal army proceeded
to occupy Macao with a view to
forestalling the French.

Native Officer,
Calcutta Native Militia,
1795.

In 1810, the depredations of
the French privateers on British commerce
demanded the capture of Mauritius (Île de
France), Bourbon and Rodrigues.   Expeditions,
in which Bombay and Madras corps and volunteer
battalions from the Bengal army took part, reduced
the islands with little difficulty.

In 1811, a large naval and military force

proceeded to capture the Island of Java from the Dutch and French. The troops included several volunteer battalions from Bengal, and some horse artillery and pioneers from Madras. The expedition met with considerable resistance, and was entirely successful. Sir Samuel Auchmuty was in command, and the famous Gillespie was one of the brigadiers. The accounts of the actions, the capture of Weltevrede and the like, read like actions of the South African War, from the well-known Dutch names which occur.

The end of the Mahratta Wars of 1803-4 meant no prolonged peace for the Indian Army. In 1814 broke out the war with Nepal due to Gurkha inroads, and after preliminary disasters was brought to a successful conclusion when General Ochterlony took the field—the terrible "Lony Ochter" of the lullaby—with fresh troops and selected generals. From this time, after the manner of the English, the conquered race was formed into soldiers, and from it spring the Gurkha battalions that are such a famous part of the Indian Army of to-day.

In 1817 two causes once more involved India in a far-reaching war. The Mahratta States, chafing under treaties, and garrisons that prevented their

overrunning the territories of their weaker neighbours, were busy planning fresh resistance, while
allied with them and even a worse evil, were the
Pindaris.   This was the name given to the
enormous bands of free-lances, who, seizing strongholds and forming centres wherever they pleased,
scourged the country round, swept and raided
where they listed, and brought half India to the
state of Europe in the days of Wallenstein and
Tilly.   These vast bodies of masterless soldiery,
chiefly horse with many odd guns, had grown from
the gradual break-up of Mogul armies, and had
continually been reinforced from Afghan tribesmen, Arabs, and any adventurous and lawless lad
who liked to hear the lark sing rather than the
mouse squeak, and they lived at their ease on the
peasantry of India.

The horror they inspired in the people has
hardly been forgotten to this day, and still perhaps
keeps the grandchildren of those who suffered,
grateful to the British who saved them.

In 1817, therefore, things had come to such a
pass, that if we were to keep India as a land for
honest men to live in, the Mahratta confederacy
must be reduced to a proper status, and the
Pindaris driven from the land.   If we realize that

the Pindaris were operating over a country about twice the size of France, and provided by nature with every kind of bolthole and fastness, we shall perhaps understand the task that Lord Moira, the Governor-General, had set himself. The combined forces of the Mahratta States and the Pindaris amounted to at least 100,000 horse, 70,000 disciplined foot, and over 500 guns. Against these, the Indian Army took the field in two large forces —the Army of the Deccan, commanded by Sir Thomas Hislop, consisting of seven divisions, and the Grand Army, commanded by the Governor-General himself, consisting of four divisions. Both armies were strong in cavalry, there being several regiments of Rohilla horse, with Gardner's and Skinner's Irregulars, and most of the regular native cavalry, as well as several regiments of British light dragoons, which were reduced in subsequent intervals of peace.

The events of this campaign are too numerous to be described in detail, but among the most famous are the defence of Seetabuldee (the Nagpore Residency), the battles of Kirkee against the Peshwa, the battle of Mahidpore against Holkar, and the famous battle of Corygaum near Poona, where the 2nd/1st Bombay Infantry (now the

JOHN
NICHOLSON

102nd Grenadiers), with 250 horse and a detachment of Madras Artillery, resisted the most desperate attacks of the whole of the Peshwa's army.
The medal to the Army of India already referred
to bears for these campaigns the clasps, "Kirkee,"
"Poona," "Kirkee and Poona," "Seetabuldee,"
"Nagpore," "Seetabuldee and Nagpore," "Maheidpoor," "Corygaum." When the main forces opposing
us had been crushed as an army in being, many weary
months followed in chasing Mahratta and Pindari
bands from one stronghold to another, and
reducing innumerable hill forts, till the land had
peace. Perhaps the feature of this war was the
increasing number of irregular horse, who proved
far the best suited to the final stage of the work,
and the subsequent attempt to improve the
organization of the army, that had shown defects
in the wide strain put on it.

It must not be supposed that in all these years
of an alien army there had not been mutinies; a
large army controlled by a trading company, with
large ideas on the subject of profits, was bound to
have passed through periods of well - founded
grievance. In 1806 had been the serious mutiny
of Vellore—that should have been as the writing
on the wall—and in 1824 the corps ordered to

Naik, Bombay Grenadier Battalion, 1801.

march to Arracan had refused to go. These will be referred to in the chapter on the Great Mutiny. In 1824 the whole of the armies were reorganized and renumbered, the double-battalion regiments being abolished, and the line in each army was renumbered from 1 upwards by single battalions, receiving their new numbers in accordance with their original date of formation. The Army of 1824, therefore, was composed as follows :—

Bengal.—Three brigades of horse artillery of four troops each, of which one troop was native. Five battalions of artillery of four companies each.

A corps of sappers and miners, with a cadre of 47 engineer officers, and a corps of pioneers.

2 battalions of European infantry.

8 regiments of light cavalry (regulars).

5 regiments of irregular horse.

68 battalions of native infantry.

Several local corps and legions.

Madras.—Two brigades of horse artillery, one European and one native.

3 battalions of foot artillery of 4 companies each, with 4 companies of lascars attached.

3 regiments of light cavalry.

2 corps of pioneers.

2 battalions of European infantry.

       52 battalions of native infantry.
       3 local battalions.

Bombay.—4 troops of horse artillery.
       8 companies of foot artillery.
       A corps of engineers and pioneers.
       3 regiments of light cavalry.
       2 regiments of irregular horse.
       2 battalions of European infantry
       24 battalions of native infantry.

It will be seen, therefore, how fast the great armies were growing, to keep pace with the territories we had acquired, and the responsibilities we had undertaken.

From the close of the Pindari wars, the expedition to Burma in 1824, and the capture of Bhurtpore, were the chief military events till we come to the First Afghan War. It will be remembered how, in 1805, Lord Lake was compelled to abandon the siege of Bhurtpore after losing 446 killed and 2479 wounded, in four separate assaults. In 1825 the insolence of the rulers of this virgin fortress knew no bounds, and circumstances forced the Government to reduce it. The Commander-in-Chief, Lord Combermere (the Stapleton Cotton of Peninsula and Waterloo fame), advanced against the place in December 1825, with a force consisting of a cavalry and two strong infantry divisions, backed up, by what Lord Lake so lacked, half the heavy guns in India. The fortress was eventually stormed, with the loss of close on 1000 killed and wounded, and a loss to the garrison computed at 8000. The prestige thus regained by the British was great, and the last clasp on the old medal was for "Bhurtpore." The Burmese War which was going on during 1825, was also commemorated by a clasp for "Ava," and its history, while devoid of large engagements, is a record of difficult and harassing operations in hill and swamp and jungle, both in Burma itself and in the Assam and Arracan districts.

About this time the whole of the infantry, including the local battalions, were clothed in scarlet with white pants, the only exception being the rifle battalions. The head-dress, though resembling a shako, was still made of black cloth on an iron, and later a wicker frame. The regular cavalry were all in French grey with various facings, the officers being dressed as dragoons, hussars or lancers. The horse artillery officers were in the English dragoon helmets, with varying crests and plumes, and the native horse artillery wore high Persian skin head-dresses. The irregular horse were in varieties of native clothing, the officers the same, though we see portraits of James Skinner, or "Old Sekunder," as he was called, at the head of his regiment dressed as an officer of dragoons.

For twelve years after the fall of Bhurtpore the army had comparative peace. As a result of the Marquis Wellesley's policy, and that followed by the Marquis of Hastings (Lord Moira) after the close of the Pindari war, there grew up many contingents paid for by the native States, but commanded by Company's officers, drilled like our own troops, and enlisting, in the case of the majority, the same races as the Bengal Army. Service in some of them was much sought after, and the Gwalior contingent came to be regarded as a *corps d'élite*, famed for its discipline and appearance.

In 1838 a policy was adopted which was to involve India in four years' war, immense disaster and chagrin, and a loss of prestige to which perhaps the Mutiny is of all causes most directly traceable. This policy consisted of forming a friendly Afghanistan to assist in opposing the advance of the Bear. The rightful ruler of Afghanistan, Shah Soojah ul Mulk, driven forth by his own folk by reason of his incompetence, was a pensioner in our midst. He had apparently sufficient following to justify our restoring him as our ally, should that course seem desirable, which to the brains of the time it did. There was no question of right or wrong. On all and every occasion Afghans had swept into Hindustan to slay, to rape, to loot, and to devastate. If, in the policy of security and good government, it was desirable to turn the tables, it was only a question of expediency and counting the cost, and the pros and cons. At any rate, to those in power the course seemed good, and the famous "Tripartite Treaty" was signed between ourselves, the Shah, and Ranjit Singh, the Maharaja of the Punjab. To place His Highness on the throne of his fathers and maintain him there, a contingent was raised in India, with British officers, of Hindustanis and Gurkhas, and to support it the Army of the Indus was collected. Since, however, the Punjab was foreign, and not too trustworthy, it was decided to advance into Afghanistan by the lengthy if easier route of Sukkur, Quetta, Kandahar, and Ghuznee. The force consisted of a brigade of cavalry, a Bengal division, a Bombay column, and the Shah's contingent, 6000 strong. The campaign that ensued, with all its successes, disappointments, disasters, and controversies cannot be discussed here. The force under Sir John Keane reached Kabul in 1839, after the successful storming of Ghuznee, and immense trouble due to want of carriage, cold and sickness, and after abandoning the useless baggage and camp followers responsible for much of the trouble. All was *couleur de rose*. The Shah sat on the throne of his fathers ; much of the army was withdrawn ; English officers rode freely over the country ; the Khyber route was opened ; ladies, children, soldiers, families, flocked to the cantonment at Kabul ; the contingent garrisoned the outposts, the brigades of occupation sat in Kabul and Kandahar. All was peace and content on the surface. We read in Sir Neville Chamberlain's life, of officers riding in from Ghuznee to Kabul for the races. The Shah was to present a medal to the troops for the storming of Ghuznee ; he had already started a magnificent order of Knighthood, the "Order of the Douranee Empire," and had conferred it on the leading lights of the army and political service, to the derision of those who did not receive it. Then came the sinister rumours, the gathering of the storm, the murder of the Envoy Sir William Macnaghten and the Envoy-elect Sir Alexander Burnes, the squabbles of an effete commander and inefficient garrison, the attempt to evacuate Kabul in the snow, the taking of hostages, and lastly, the massacre of half-frozen troops and frost-bitten followers—such a disaster and humiliation as had never before happened to British arms. Bright spots there were. The defence of Kelat-i-Ghilzai by the 3rd Shah's, now the 12th (Kelat-i-Ghilzai) Regiment, under Captain Craigie, with a few European artillerymen, the defence of Jellalabad by Sale and the " Illustrious garrison," the sturdy demeanour of Nott at Kandahar, with his " splendid Sepoy regiments," all were bright spots, to redeem incompetence and pusillanimity. But the world looked at the failure; a British brigade annihilated under most pitiable circumstances was what the Eastern world saw, and rejoiced at. Then came the avenging army under Pollock, with trembling sepoys to be heartened and redisciplined at Peshawar, and a final advance, not so much to rescue the English men and women in captivity as to help the sturdy Nott, who had agreed with Pollock to carry out the orders to evacuate Afghanistan by coming *via* Kabul on their joint responsibility. This method of evacuating Afghanistan enabled vengeance to be taken on the guilty capital, and the British prisoners to be rescued. Besides the medal for the storming of Ghuznee in the first phase, special medals were given for the defence of Kelat-i-Ghilzai and Jellalabad respectively, and another to the avenging armies, bearing the inscription "Victoria Vindex." The armies of Nott and Pollock then marched down from Kabul, and after traversing an almost hostile Punjab, passed the British frontier into Ferozepore, to find an immense reception awaiting them from the Governor-General, Lord Ellenborough, at the head of a reserve army. An interesting incident of the times, was the intense camaraderie between the 13th Foot and the 35th Bengal Native Infantry, parts of the "Illustrious garrison," which ended in the whole of the latter feasting their British comrades before parting at Ferozepore. Even the 35th, however, went under in '57, and with them the battery of artillery on whose guns Lord Ellenborough had engraved a mural crown for its share in the defence. Despite, however, the triumphant finale, the maimed and frost-bitten remnants of the earlier occupation, rescued from begging in the Kabul bazaars, told a tale of lessened prestige that was not forgotten for many years.

During the strain of the Afghan War, however, India was still able to find troops for Imperial oversea purposes.   In 1840, a large amount of British property had been destroyed by the Chinese in an attempt to solve by a short cut the opium

A Grenadier Sepoy of 30th Regiment of Bengal Native Infantry, 1815.

problem, and an expedition under Sir Hugh Gough was sent to South China.   The major portion of the force were troops of the Madras Line, for, as it had become a habit for the Bengal Army not to cross the seas, the usual volunteer battalions alone represented the Bengal Army.

An aftermath of the Afghan wars was the trouble in Scinde, ending in Sir Charles Napier's short and famous campaign, in which three Bombay Cavalry and two Bombay Infantry regiments took part with the 22nd Foot.   The annexation of Scinde that followed, still further extended the responsibilities of the sepoy army, and necessitated more battalions.

This same year, 1843, was to see an important though short campaign in internal India.   A minority in Scindia's domain, the State of Gwalior, had resulted in dissensions between two factions.

The army took opposite sides to that supported by Government, and the army was a very considerable force, still retaining the European organization and drill that it had learnt in the days of De Boigne and his successors.   Gwalior was a large Hindu State, and there was considerable danger of an attempt to combine with the other great Hindu power, the Sikhs of the Punjab.   To obviate any outbreak of the Gwalior troops, an army of exercise was collected as a precautionary measure near Agra, and another force at Jhansi.   Eventually the state of affairs at Gwalior necessitated a move of the British troops on the capital, but it was not expected to be more than a promenade, and some ladies even accompanied the force.   While Sir Hugh Gough advanced from Muttra, Sir John Grey advanced from Jhansi, and to every one's surprise, the Mahratta army was found in position near Maharajpore, and also at Punniar.   The former force opened fire on Sir Hugh Gough, and a severe engagement ensued, in which the Gwalior artillery was especially well served.   The battle at Punniar was also a severe one, though on a lesser scale.   These two victories, however, completed the overthrow of the Gwalior troops and ended the disturbing conditions in the Durbar.   A six-pointed bronze star was awarded the troops, with a silver centre, and the words " Maharajpore " and " Punniar " respectively in the centre.

In the winter of 1845 the most serious trouble that had threatened India for many years came to a head. The Sikhs, who had lost the firm hand of the sagacious Ranjit Singh, and were burning to invade British India, finally crossed the Sutlej in large numbers near Ferozepore. The Sutlej campaign with its hard-fought battles, its vicissitudes and successful conclusion, is a story by itself, and has often been told from many points of view. The native troops that took part in the campaign were entirely from Bengal, and acquitted themselves with varying credit. The Sikhs were far the severest foe that had been met in India, and the climate was rigorous to natives of Hindustan, while there was considerable feeling towards the last Hindu State. The bulk of the fighting fell on the European troops, whose casualties were very severe.

Large additions were made to the army at the outbreak of the campaign, including the formation of eight more regiments of cavalry. The cantoning of a force of occupation at Lahore during the minority of the young Maharaja, put some strain on the army, and a special force was raised for the garrisoning of the Jullundur Doab.

The attempt to bolster up the Sikh State, that was adopted as a definite policy after the First Sikh War, was soon doomed to failure. The Sikhs had not yet made up their minds to accept even British domination, and an outburst was precipitated by the murder, at Mooltan, of two British officers lent to the Durbar. This took place in the early summer of 1848, and it was some time before a force for the reduction of Mooltan, into which Mool Raj, the rebellious Sikh governor, had thrown himself, could be assembled. Events, too, soon showed that the outbreak at Mooltan was likely to become general, and a large army was organized at Ferozepore, consisting of four brigades of cavalry and three divisions of infantry.

The reinforcement of the force attacking Mooltan, by a Bombay brigade, the final capture of the fortress, the passing of the Chenab, the hard-fought battle of Chillianwalla, the final crushing of the Sikhs at Gujarat, and the surrender of the Sirdars and their followers at Rawalpindi, with the pursuit of the Afghan horse to the Khyber, are all matters of history and of full record.

Suffice it here to say that the Bengal native army formed the bulk of the force, reinforced for the crowning victory of Gujarat by the Bombay brigade that had taken part in the storm of Mooltan. The brunt of the heavy fighting in this war fell as usual on the European troops, but some of the native infantry corps were especially distinguished and suffered very heavy casualties. The losses sustained by the British troops in these two Sikh wars were very severe, far more so than any portion, especially the native infantry, had been accustomed to experience for many years.

The annexation of the Punjab was followed by more additions to the native army, with very little corresponding increase in the European garrison, while the exigencies of holding the immense area annexed, and of watching the Afghan frontier, demanded a grouping of the European troops in the North of India, and a very large native garrison. The frontier brigade organized in the Jullundur Doab was moved to the Afghan border, and from it, with the addition of several new corps, recruited largely from the Khalsa regiments that had been disbanded, the Punjab Irregular Force was formed, which, known later as the Punjab Frontier Force, has become so famous a portion of the Indian

Army. Lord Dalhousie's policy of annexing States in hopeless anarchy, or which had no successor in heredity on the demise of the reigning chief, added considerably to the demands on the native force in the country.

In 1854 the annexation of Nagpore necessitated the formation of a local force, and the annexation of Oudh in 1856 was perforce followed by the immediate formation of the Oudh Irregular Force. It should be realized that the state of the country, with its poor communications and immense hilly and jungle tracts, demanded far more effective forces than police, for the ordinary pacification and maintenance of order in the districts. In countries where might had been right for perhaps a couple of hundred years, and the hand alone had kept the head since the memory of man, there were scores of reiving barons and robber chiefs to be dealt with. To make the barons and their retainers pay revenue, obey the law, and cease to spoil the peasant and the trader, was for many years beyond the power of mere police, and it was this need, coupled with the fact that revenue was by no means ample, that demanded troops, and those of the cheaper, or native, kind. The policy, therefore, dangerous though it seemed, was an almost unavoidable one, given the conditions as they appeared to men at the time.

The war in the Crimea had withdrawn some European troops from India which had not been replaced in 1857. The Second Burmese War, unavoidably thrust on us in 1853, had called for still more troops of occupation, and in 1856, a Persian expedition removed several European corps for the time beyond the seas. Several native corps of the Bombay Army took part in the Persian expedition and gained considerable distinction. Between 1849 and 1857 the new frontier at the foot of the Afghan hills gave much trouble, and numerous small frontier expeditions, to impress the laws of *meum* and *tuum* on the tribes, were necessary.

The foregoing in brief is the outline of the causes which gradually formed the huge Indian Army, and of the magnitude and the vastness of the services it rendered both in India and in the Empire generally. Minor infidelities and mutinies there had been, and many failings of the service as a whole had been often pointed out, with many aberrations of judgment on the part of the administration. The fact remains, however, that come rain come shine, this vast alien force had, for a hundred and fifty years, rendered the most faithful military service to their masters, while an immense feeling of attachment had grown up between officers and men. So much so that when the storm came, the retired officers from India could not credit the news. "What! dear old Jack mutiny, kill his sahibs, murder their families—impossible!" Such were the views of the mass of officers who had spent happy and often glorious careers with the sepoy regiments. However, blow up that sepoy army did, with all the romance and tragedy and inconsequence imaginable; and to understand in outline how and why it did so, is essential to a right understanding of the conditions of to-day. The Indian Army, as we now know it, is the result of the evolution of the portion of the army that remained faithful, and the reconstruction of that that fell away.

That great army stood in 1857 at 311,538 (Imperial Gazetteer), with 39,500 Europeans, King's and Company's. It was, too, dressed and equipped for the most part on a pedantic model of the British Army. In the great lines of battle drawn up to meet the Sikhs, the European and Native Infantry were dressed in their scarlet coatees and white ducks, with tall black shakos and white buff cross-belts. The artillery and cavalry, other than the irregulars, were also dressed much as their European brethren. For the most part, too, corps fought in their full dress, after the manner of the time. The 24th Foot at Chillian-walla, for instance, had their shakos pulled off forcing their way through the thorn jungle to get at the Sikh guns. Some corps, like the 61st Foot, however, went into action in shell-jackets and forage-caps with white covers. How this enormous army, in its European costume of coatee and shako, came to mutiny and rue untold, and how the modern army grew up in its place, will be outlined in the following chapters.

CHAPTER II

THE TWO GREAT MAHRATTA WARS

In the foregoing chapter, the history of the army from its inception to the Mutiny has been run through in outline. Allusion has been made to the great campaigns, but to describe these in detail and write a history of the wars of the Company's Army would require many volumes. Nor is it possible to dwell on the exploits of the native regiments, and the actions in which they individually came to fame, even if this were confined to those that still figure on the Army List. There are, however, two great campaigns in the early portion of the nineteenth century which are specially remarkable, and which, more than any others, formed the real India of to-day, and resulted in that consolidated Indian Army which lasted till 1857 in Bengal, and practically to this day in the other Presidencies.

These campaigns are the two great Mahratta wars, of which the first lasted from 1803 to 1806, and included the famous battles of Sir Arthur Wellesley and Lord Lake ; and the latter, from 1817 to 1819, represented the final conclusions with the Mahrattas, and the ridding of the country from the scourge of the Pindari bands of free-lances and robbers. The Sikh wars and the First Afghan War are well known from the many histories and biographies that bear on them. These two Mahratta campaigns, however, are little known, yet many of the most famous battle honours of the surviving Company's regiments, as well as those of the British Line, are derived from them.

The enemy who fought against us were principally the Mahratta chiefs, who controlled immense bands of mercenary horse and foot, largely trained and officered by Frenchmen, and comprising every lawless man in the country-side, with Persians, Arabs, Afghans, and even negroes. There was no case of the patriot fighting for his country-side, and the campaigns have, to a great extent, but confined the Mahratta chiefs to their rightful provinces, and curbed the immense pretensions and scrambling conquests that had ensued on the collapse of the Mogul Empire. The country-side only longed for deliverance from an era like to the worst days of the Palatinate.

The daring of some of these troops is clearly evinced in the casualties that they inflicted on the victorious British, while the political conceptions of some of the chiefs were magnificent. None of them, however, possessed the power to consolidate a Hindu rule, and their pretensions resulted in constant devastation of their neighbours' or rivals' territories, including our own.

The result of these campaigns brought the British paramount to the borders of the Punjab, bestowed peace on millions of people, and gave our own territories, for the first time, complete immunity from cruel raids. Incidentally, it broke the fortunes of many of the barons who lived by raiding and pillage and adventurer service, and of the thousands of hereditary and mercenary soldiers for whom there was no place in our ranks. Several thousands were absorbed in our irregulars, but the remainder had, perforce, to turn peasant.

The campaigns that brought this about it is now proposed briefly to describe, as a fitting complement to the outline history of the Company's Army, more especially as in these extremely arduous campaigns the backing of British troops was far smaller than in later years. Some of the events, too, such as the defence of Seetabuldee and the fight at Corygaum, both in 1817, against overwhelming odds, with only a small force of European artillery in the way of backing, are among the most famous events in the whole military history of our Empire.

The First Mahratta War, 1803-6

The history of the Governor-Generalship of Lord Mornington, afterwards the Marquis Wellesley, is one of struggle against the French influence in India, as revived by the plans and ambitions of the Emperor Napoleon, and against the hostility of the Mahratta princes. When Sivaji, the Mahratta prince and leader known to the Moguls as "the mountain rat," had established his Hindu kingdom among the mountains of Western India, he had formed a barrier to the power of Islam and its proselytizing influence which at first had promised to revive some of the glories of the old Hindu rule in India. On his death, however, the solidarity of the Mahrattas soon passed away. The nominal sovereignty remained in the hands of the Rajas of Satara, but the high officers of state soon raised semi-independent principalities for themselves. The Rajas of Satara exercised nominal control through their Peshwa or hereditary minister of the crown, who soon also became a territorial ruler. The Mahratta princes, of whom the principal were Scindia, whose capital was Gwalior; Holkar, the ruler of Indore; the Bhonsla at Nagpore, together with the Peshwa at Poona, were always at war with their neighbours in some form of confederacy, or else individually among themselves. Combined against the Mogul power, against the Nizam, or against the British, fighting the Rajput princes, and scouring the territories of their neighbours with hordes of horse, they and their name had been a horror and offence in the land for generations.

The first steps necessary to counteract the French influence had been to destroy, once and for all, the cruel and impossible ruler of Mysore, Tippoo Sultan, son of the great Hyder Ali. The history of his and his father's wars with the British, and his own implacable and unreasoning behaviour, had resulted, as has been related in the previous chapter, in his death at the final storming and capture of Seringapatam. In Hyderabad the Nizam had a force of 15,000 men trained by M. Raymond, and officered by many of the

French officers left out of employment when the French power had died out, and reinforced by officers from Europe. Some were royalist refugees, others sent by Napoleon to push French influence. The Governor-General insisted, as a price of his protection of the Nizam against the demands and invasions of the Mahrattas, that this force should be disbanded and replaced by a British subsidiary force. To fortify the Nizam in his resolution, four Madras battalions and some guns marched into Hyderabad, and the French-trained force was disbanded, the officers coming to the British for protection, and many of the men re-enlisting in the British service. This took place at the end of 1798.

The ground was now clear for compelling the Mahratta princes to enter into agreement with the British, to cease from attack and raid on British territory and that of its allies, and combine for the defence of Hindustan against the Afghan invader.

For several years after the death of the Peshwa Madho Rao, intrigue and counter - intrigue, killings, poisonings, and inter-Mahratta battlings with European leaders on each side, had torn the States to distraction. At last, in 1802, Jeswant

Rao Holkar defeated the joint forces of the Peshwa and Scindia close to Poona, and Bajee Rao, the former, fled to British territory and signed the Treaty of Bassein, whereby he vowed alliance with the British, in return for a subsidiary force of some European artillery and six battalions of sepoys to protect him in his capital.

The other Mahratta chiefs were much incensed at the Peshwa's defection from the cause of independent and combined hostility to all and every neighbour. For twenty-five years the confederacy had avoided all foreign alliances, and now the head of them had accepted it. Holkar proclaimed Bajee Rao's brother, Amrut Rao, Peshwa in his stead, and it became necessary for us to support Bajee Rao, and generally obtain some settlement.

The foregoing description is necessary to understand the situation that brought General Arthur Wellesley in the Deccan and General Lake, the Commander-in-Chief in Hindustan, into the field for the campaign that practically made the modern India.

The British had been organizing for some time for a war that was obviously inevitable. The theatre of war was enormous, and necessitated the employment of several entirely separate forces.

The Army of the Deccan

General Wellesley advanced on Poona with 8000 foot, 1700 cavalry, and 2000 Mysore horse from Mysore, through the Southern Mahratta States, to reinstate the Peshwa, bringing in his train many Mahratta chieftains to support their head. Colonel Stevenson came up with the Subsidiary Force, and the Nizam's troops from Hyderabad, the latter numbering 9000 horse and 6000 foot.

The Commander-in-Chief advanced with 10,500 men on Delhi, leaving 3500 in reserve at Allahabad. Eight thousand men under General Stuart moved into the Southern Mahratta States, and 8000 under Colonel Murray entered Gujarat. Five thousand were also sent towards Cuttack, which province was held by the Bhonsla (the Raja of Berar). The British force totalled 50,000 men, which was far larger than any hitherto put into the field.

Assaye

The first move consisted of a forced march, to save Poona from being burned by Holkar. General Wellesley then stormed the town and powerful fortress of Ahmednagar, which became an excellent base to store his reserve supplies. The storming of the town wall was a remarkable feat, and cost 169 men; while the fort, one of the strongest in India, surrendered after two days' bombardment. It is not possible to follow the details of the campaign, but suffice it to say that General Wellesley shortly after found himself in a position to strike at the combined forces of Scindia and the Bhonsla near Jalna, in the territory of Aurunga-bad, with the troops under his immediate command. Swollen rivers prevented Colonel Stevenson from joining him, though only a few miles off, and Wellesley found himself in front of some 55,000 Mahrattas, posted in the fork of two rivers, the Jua and the Kelna, the swollen Kelna being a mile in front of their position. Scindia and the Bhonsla had with them a magnificent park of artillery, massed in the vicinity of the village of Assaye.

The enemy's position indicated no particular desire to come to action for the time being, but the opportunity was too good to be missed, despite the fact that the British numbered but 4500.

With that audacity which has never failed the combatant in the East who is ready to grasp the nettle danger with the hand of courage, the British leader decided to attack. How to get at the enemy was the difficulty, for at present their line faced him, with a swollen and unfordable river in their front. The quick eye of General Wellesley, however, showed him two villages opposite each other on the river, which, he felt, must mean a practicable ford. The British were at once moved in that direction, and succeeded in crossing, to find that the enemy, pivoted on the village of Assaye, had changed front half left to meet them.

The total number of the British was but 4500, of whom some 2200 were cavalry. This small force, immediately it could form up, advanced with enthusiasm on the enormous force of the Mahrattas, and their immense line of artillery. The enemy's infantry included 116 regular battalions, 600 men of M. Pohlman's brigade, and 2500 of M. Dupont. Four battalions belonging to the Begum Sumru were also present. The impetuosity of the British attack resulted in a determined counter-attack by the rallied enemy and the descent of their cavalry, only driven off by determined charges of the British dragoons and native cavalry. After three hours, however, the enemy were in full flight, leaving 1200 dead and 98 guns on the field.

The British casualties were over 2000, in which

all corps shared heavily. The 74th Foot lost the most, with 10 officers killed and 6 wounded, and rank and file in proportion, while the 1/4th and 2/12th battalions of Madras native infantry lost heavily also. The native corps that took part were a party of Madras sappers, the 4th, 5th, and 7th Native Cavalry, and the 1/2nd, 1/4th, 1/8th, 1/10th, 2/12th battalions and the Pioneers. Of these only three are still in the service, besides the sappers, viz. the 1/2nd, now the 62nd Punjabis; the 1/4th, now the 64th Pioneers; and the 2/12th, now the 84th Punjabis. The present 63rd Palamcottah Light Infantry and 73rd Carnatic Infantry were with Wellesley at Ahmednagar, while the present 66th, 79th, 80th, 81st, and 82nd were with Colonel Stevenson's force a few miles from Assaye. It will be seen that it was the old Madras Line, then at the zenith of its fame, which formed the entire native portion of the victorious army in the Deccan. The reductions that the piping times of peace have necessitated have unfortunately removed from the Army List all the corps of Madras cavalry that gained such fame in this campaign, as well as H.M. 19th Light Dragoons.

After Assaye, Colonel Stevenson moved on to capture the immense hill-fortress of Aseergurh, then belonging to Scindia, which eventually capitulated. During these operations several French officers and non-commissioned officers surrendered on various occasions. Some had already been found dead after different engagements, an officer of high rank being found on the field of Assaye.

ARGAUM

After reforming his force that had fought at Assaye, General Wellesley moved on to complete the overthrow of the Bhonsla's forces, as Scindia had arranged an armistice pending negotiations. On the 28th of November Wellesley, having joined with Stevenson for the purpose of moving on the strong hill-fort of Gawilgurh, in the north of Berar, came on a large force of the Bhonsla's and Scindia's troops drawn up at the village of Argaum. The troops of Scindia were there in contravention of the armistice, and though late in the day, the General decided to attack. The enemy's position was five miles long, and his force included large numbers of Persian and Arab mercenaries. The fighting was desperate, the 1/6th Madras native infantry, now the 66th Punjabis, repulsing an overwhelming charge of Scindia's horse. The fire from the heavy batteries of the Mahrattas, however, succeeded in disorganizing many of the native troops at the earlier stages, and it was not till late in the evening that the enemy were in full flight, with the loss of much of their camp and treasure and 38 guns. The British loss was 346 all told.

Gawilgurh

From Argaum, Wellesley pushed on at once to the Bhonsla's fort of Gawilgurh. On the 12th of December breaching batteries were opened, and the place was stormed on the 14th, in the face of determined opposition. Our losses amounted to 146.

The storming of Ahmednagar, the battles of Assaye and Argaum, and the capture of the impregnable fortresses of Aseergurh and Gawilgurh, were the main features of General Wellesley's campaign, and were followed by overtures for peace on practically our own terms. They were all operations of more than usual severity. The battle of Assaye was as desperate as any in our history, and full in its promise of the power of leading, possessed by the newly discovered " Sepoy General." The casualties, in their proportion to

the size of the force, were as heavy as any on
record.   When, close on half a century later, the
British Government came to make up its jewels
and award medals for half-forgotten services,
clasps for all these actions, except Ahmednagar,
were added to the medal "To the army in India."
They have been described in some detail here,
because it was in this war and that of 1817 that
the real Indian Empire was founded, by the old
Indian Army, and the corps that took so con-
tinuous a share in the campaign in the Deccan
still survive intact.

THE GRAND ARMY

The other campaign of the same war, that
conducted by Lord Lake himself, equally famous,
was so far as the Indian Army is concerned chiefly
the work of corps lost in the cataclysm of '57.
There are, however, still four corps on the rolls of
the army who marched with the Commander-in-
Chief, and a briefer outline of this phase of the
war is therefore desirable for the glory of Jack
Sepoy and the famous 76th Foot, who formed the
kernel of this sledge-hammer army.   The Indian
corps who remain are the 1st Cavalry (Skinner's
Horse), the 1st Brahmans (then the 1/9th of the

Bengal Line), the 2nd Queen's Own Rajput Light Infantry (then the 2/15th), and the 4th Prince Albert Victor's Rajputs (then the 2/16th).

The Grand Army had been assembling at Kanauj, where the large force of cavalry, three regiments of dragoons, and five regiments of native cavalry had been exercised together for some months and trained as a division. It was here that the first horse artillery was formed, by attaching two six-pounder galloper guns to each cavalry regiment. The infantry of the force consisted of one European battalion, the 76th, and eleven native battalions.

17th Regiment Bengal Irregular Cavalry, 1850.

The immediate object was the destruction of the large force belonging to Scindia, which was disciplined under M. Perron, the successor of De Boigne. This force numbered nine brigades, with a total of 43,000 men and 464 guns. It was maintained by the revenue of what was known as "The French State," being the Doab between the Ganges and the Jumna. This had been assigned to the administration of De Boigne and Perron, to defray the cost of the force and the pay of the Europeans. In August the Grand Army slowly moved up towards the Mahratta frontier, and on the 28th was at Coel, within a few miles of M. Perron's army at Alligurh. A regular advance of the army on the 29th so impressed the Mahrattas that General Perron moved off after a skirmish to Delhi, leaving a Colonel Pedron in the fort of Alligurh.

ALLIGURH

As Alligurh was General Perron's headquarters, in which he had built his barracks and stores, it was decided to storm it at once, in spite of its twice triple series of gates and bastions. The assault was made early on the 4th of September, and carried with a loss of 260 killed and wounded, in which the 76th Foot, who were always to bear the brunt of all Lake's battles, lost 5 officers and 19 rank and file killed, and 4 officers and 62 rank and file wounded, the 1/4th Native Infantry losing almost as many, including 1 British officer killed and 4 wounded. The enemy's loss was very heavy. M.

Pedron was captured, with 281 guns of all kinds, and large quantities of sepoys' uniform of French pattern.

BATTLE OF DELHI

No time was lost in following the enemy to Delhi, but General Perron himself rode in with some of his European officers, to surrender, before another battle took place. On the 16th of September, after a march of 18 miles, Lord Lake's force were pitching their camp near the Hindun river, a few miles from Delhi, when they found the Mahrattas, numbering sixteen of M. Louis Bourquien's regular battalions, and several thousand horse with plenty of artillery, were drawn up within a mile or so of them, hidden by long grass. Their guns soon opened on the British outposts. Lord Lake decided to attack at once, and did so, himself leading the attack. The furious and ordered attack of the British into the teeth of the Mahratta artillery fire was irresistible, and the whole of the enemy were routed with severe loss, and all the regulars, except two battalions, cut up. Sixty-three guns were captured, with a considerable amount of treasure. The British loss was 477, of which the 76th, as usual, lost the most (137);

and the 2/4th Native Infantry again suffered nearly as heavily, while the 2/15th, now the 2nd Rajputs, the only corps of the Indian Army taking part in this battle that is still extant, lost an officer and 16 men killed and 9 men wounded.

The next day Lord Lake entered Delhi, and rescued the Mogul Emperor, the blind Shah Alam, from his Mahratta jailors, who, while ruling under his seal, maintained him in poverty and squalor. On the 19th M. Bourquien and four of his officers surrendered, anxious for protection against the people of Delhi. After leaving a garrison at Delhi, and arranging treaties with minor chiefs, the British Army returned south towards Agra, to capture that stronghold, which still maintained many regular troops, and the gun foundry, where a Scotchman turned out many of the numerous guns in the Mahratta hands. *En route*, a treaty of alliance was concluded with the Jat Raja of Bhurtpore. On arrival before Agra, the fort and garrison were summoned to surrender; and on refusing, the force of several battalions camped on the glacis were attacked and dispersed or driven within the huge sandstone bastions. Twenty-six guns were taken, the British loss amounting to 228. The 2/9th, now the 1st Brahmans; the

2/15th, now the 2nd Rajputs; and the 1/16th, now the 4th Rajputs, took part in these operations, the 2/9th having two British officers killed.

After some negotiations Colonel Sutherland, the commandant of the fortress, completed arrangements for a surrender, which included 164 guns, and all the stores in this immense stronghold and palace. The great gun of Agra, weighing 96,600 pounds, with a calibre of 23 inches, was among the trophies.

LASWARRIE

Still a further portion of Scindia's organized forces required to be dealt with. Some battalions which had escaped from Delhi, and the Chevalier Dudrenac's brigades which had come up from the Deccan, had taken post on the flank of our communications with Delhi, and needed attention. The Chevalier himself, with two officers, had surrendered shortly before Lord Lake's arrival at Agra. The Governor-General had issued a proclamation calling on foreign and British (European) subjects now serving with the hostile States to leave their service, promising safe conduct and protection for their property, and many were availing themselves of this offer, hastened by the fact that in several cases the troops had turned on their officers and murdered them.

On the 27th of October 1803 Lake marched from Agra in the direction of Deig. Lake himself, anxious to bring the enemy to battle and end the campaign, pushed on ahead with the cavalry division of three regiments of dragoons and five of native cavalry. On November 1, in the early morning, hearing that the enemy were at Laswarrie, he pushed on, covering the 25 miles in six hours, the infantry following behind. Before the day was far advanced the cavalry came up with the enemy and at once closed, with the object of, at any rate, forcing the Mahrattas to keep their ground. The enemy deployed an enormous line of guns linked with chains, but up and down and through this the eight regiments charged, and charged again. The British dragoons lost 8 officers and 34 men killed, and 19 officers and 89 men wounded, and 310 horses. The native cavalry lost 1 officer killed and 5 wounded, with 17 troopers killed and 69 wounded, and 172 horses. No better instance of the cavalry spirit can be quoted, and it was rewarded with entire success. The enemy changed position slightly, and formed again for battle. By noon up marched the unfailing infantry, done to a turn, but ready for more. They had marched 65 miles in forty-eight hours, while the cavalry had done 45 miles in twenty-four hours.

After a short halt the whole force went into battle in the full heat of the sun. The enemy's cannonade was terrific, and by evening the British losses had totalled 834, but the whole of the Mahratta army was destroyed, large numbers killed and many prisoners, and 71 guns were taken. The 76th lost 2 officers and 41 men killed, and 4 officers and 170 men wounded. The 2/12th N.I. also lost heavily. The 1st Brahmans, the 2nd Rajputs, and the 4th Rajputs took part, under their old numbers losing 16, 37, and 87 respectively of all ranks killed and wounded.

The victory of Laswarrie would have closed this phase of the campaign but for the activity of Holkar. Scindia, the Bhonsla, the Raja of Bhurtpore, and most of the minor Rajas had now entered into offensive and defensive alliances with the British, as a result of this and Wellesley's campaign. The forces in Cuttack and Bundelkhund had been equally successful. In the former campaign some Madras native infantry had taken part, of which the present 69th Punjabis are the sole survivors. Gwalior, Scindia's capital, had been reduced, in which service the present 1st Brahmans also shared, and the troops had some hopes of going into summer quarters to escape the daily growing heat. The attitude of Holkar, however, in threatening the Doab, and endeavouring to stir up the chiefs who had made peace, necessitated one more effort, and Lord Lake in person made an advance in force towards Holkar. This campaign involved many minor actions, and much skirmishing with the Mewatis in the broken country between Agra and Rajputana, but without any opportunity offering of bringing Holkar and his main forces to book.

Summer of 1804

At last the army withdrew towards the Jumna, and moved into cantonments, after enduring heavy losses, especially among the Europeans, from the intense heat. Many corps did not get into quarters till the commencement of the rains. To cover the Doab, Colonel Monson was left on the Chumbal with a considerable detachment.

Monson's Retreat

It was this detachment which was to experience the first real disaster to British arms in India, and which was to prolong the war to 1806. In July the news that Holkar had advanced, induced Colonel Monson to leave his camp and move to meet him. As Holkar withdrew Monson followed for many marches, till, fearful for his supplies and communications, he decided to fall back. This was the signal for the advance of vast hordes of the enemy, and for the general hostility of all those through whose country he passed. Want of supplies and swollen rivers reduced the troops to the greatest straits, and though fighting constantly, demoralization at last set in, and the force, entirely native, at last fell to pieces, the survivors arriving by detachments at the British border. Of the five infantry battalions composing the force, the 2/21st, a newly raised battalion, did well (now the 5th Light Infantry), and is the only survivor on the Army List.

DEFENCE OF DELHI

The news of this disaster to the invincible English spread rapidly. Lord Lake at once took steps to collect the army from its summer quarters, and on the 1st of October advanced towards Muttra from the vicinity of Agra. Holkar had already occupied Muttra. As the British advanced the Mahrattas fell back, always refusing an engagement, and it then became known that his regular infantry were besieging Delhi. The Commander-in-Chief at once pressed on to the relief, regardless of the swarms of horse who harassed flanks and rear. The Mahratta force had appeared before Delhi on the 7th of October, but Colonel Ochterlony, the Resident, had already summoned in Colonel Burns' corps and several detachments of local troops, and managed to hold certain portions of the dilapidated and lengthy bastioned wall. Heavy breaching batteries were brought against the wall, and a hot cannonade kept up. The crumbling walls were, however, repaired at night, and the garrison, always on the alert, made continual sorties. The enemy, however, after being repulsed in an assault on the 14th, disappeared on the 15th as suddenly as they had come, and shortly after Lord Lake marched up.

Lake's Pursuit of Holkar

It was then discovered that Holkar was making for the Doab to ravage our territories, so after him marched Lake himself with the three dragoon regiments (8th, 27th, and 29th) and two regiments of native cavalry. General Fraser followed with the main body of the force. Lake's pursuit of Holkar is one of the great cavalry feats of history, and it was not till 350 miles had been traversed in the short space of a fortnight, that, marching all night, Holkar's cavalry camp was ridden down at dawn by a charge of the British force, which destroyed a large number of his horse, took many prisoners and all his guns and baggage, and almost got that desperate Mahratta himself.

BATTLE OF DEIG

In the meantime General Fraser, marching south, came up with Holkar's infantry and guns underneath the walls of the fort of Deig, in the territory of the Raja of Bhurtpore. This force consisted of 24 regular battalions with 160 guns and some irregular horse. The usual audacious attack on the part of the British followed, led also, as usual, by the 76th. The enemy were completely overthrown with the loss of 87 of their guns. The British loss was 643. The 2nd Rajputs (2/15th) took part, losing a British officer killed and another wounded. General Fraser himself was mortally wounded, and Colonel Monson brought the battle to its victorious close.

Capture of Deig

The battle of Deig, however, was by no means the last that the British were to see of the place. It belonged to Bhurtpore, and as an aftermath of the Monson disaster, our ally of Bhurtpore had fallen away from his agreement. The fortress of Deig opened its gates to Holkar's troops after the battle, as did also Bhurtpore itself. As the land could have no rest so long as Holkar was burning and slaying all and sundry, with friendly haunts to do it from, it was necessary to reduce Deig. On the 11th of December the British appeared before the walls. On the 24th the breaches were ready, and by dawn on Christmas Day the place was ours, with the loss of 43 killed and 184 wounded. A hundred cannon of sorts were taken.

Siege of Bhurtpore

Next to reckon with was Bhurtpore itself. By this time the army with Lord Lake had been considerably reinforced, and shattered troops relieved by fresh ones, saving always the 76th, whom nothing daunted, and the dragoon regiments. On the 1st of January 1805 the British encamped before the virgin fortress, which was protected by immense commanding bastions of solid mud.   Not all the daring of the 76th, however, nor the devotion of their native comrades, was to put Lord Lake inside Bhurtpore.   Two assaults were repulsed with appalling loss.   Then there arrived a division of Bombay troops under General Jones.   With it were the 2/1st, the 2/2nd, the 1/3rd, and the 1/9th of the Bombay Line, now the 101st Grenadiers, the 104th Rifles, the 105th and 117th Mahrattas.   The new troops were burning for action.   Another determined attempt to storm failed hopelessly, though again and again daring spirits carried the colours up the breach.   Still a fourth and larger attempt was made, and then the force stood back, having lost 103 officers and 3100 men.

Summer of 1805

Immense preparations were made for a blockade and prolonged siege, while various forces moved against bodies of Holkar's horse that threatened communications or ravaged the Doab.   In the meantime the Raja of Bhurtpore sued for peace, which was made on reasonable terms.   The diminished but still jaunty army then moved off to clear Bundelkhund of Mahrattas, and finally went into summer quarters about Agra and Muttra   Holkar still being at large, though with his forces for the time being dissipated. The three regiments of dragoons, it is recorded, spent the rains in the immense courts of Akbar's tomb at Sekundra, near Agra, the officers and their families occupying the tombs of the Omras round, as their dwellings. Many troops were cantoned at Fattehpur Sikri.

The Pursuit of Holkar to the Punjab

As the rains passed the activity of Holkar became more marked, and was having its influence on Scindia. Finally, Holkar made his way towards the Punjab, with a view of inducing the Sikhs to overrun the Doab with him. The year before, Lord Lake had had to drive large bodies of Sikhs from the vicinity of Delhi, and the possibility of a Hindu combination of this nature was very serious. So in October 1805 once again the Grand Army had to take the field, and marched north from Agra and Cawnpore and Muttra, two brigades of cavalry and one of infantry leading. This force marched straight past Delhi, after Holkar, to the banks of the Beas, where it halted, Holkar being with the Sikhs at Amritsar. This display of force resulted in the Sikhs refusing to support Holkar, and, after much negotiation, a treaty with Scindia and Holkar on a reasonably satisfactory basis being concluded. In January 1806 the war-worn army commenced its march south, and the Great Mahratta war of three years was at an end. The Marquis Wellesley, who had conducted affairs through so many stirring years, had returned home, and a change of policy had taken place, on account of which possibly another Mahratta war was yet to come. And in the years to follow, the hordes of the Pindaris were much reinforced by the disbanded soldiery of this war.

The medal to the Army of India, awarded to the survivors half a century later, recognized the campaigns of Lord Lake by clasps for " Capture of Alligurh," " Battle of Delhi," " Defence of Delhi," " Laswarrie," " Battle of Deig," " Capture of Deig." Bhurtpore, the most desperate business of the lot, was not of course rewarded, since the fortress never fell, till Lord Combermere captured it in 1825, for which capture the medal bears the clasp " Bhurtpore."

THE MAHRATTA AND PINDARI WAR, 1817-19

The reversal of policy that had followed the successes of Lake and Wellesley had prevented anything approaching a permanent settlement. The Mahratta chiefs were continually intriguing, while the Pindari bands, bandits of every race and tribe, originally formed on the break-up of the Mogul armies, had grown to enormous size. They were overrunning the whole of Hindustan, far down into the British provinces, with fire and sword and torture. In 1817 things had come to such a pass that it was decided to organize a vast force, and tramp out the immense area involved. The Marquis of Hastings, the Governor-General, called on the Mahratta chiefs to aid him against the common enemy, but received little more than promises. The general plan of operations was to advance from all sides on the fastnesses bordering the banks of the river Narbudda, at the foot of the Vindhya Mountains, along which the Pindaris had long established their centres. The forces of Holkar, Scindia, the Peshwa, and the Bhonsla were to be watched at the same time, lest they, too, should elect to side against the cause of law and order.

Two large armies were formed, the Grand Army of four divisions which assembled at Cawnpore under the Governor-General himself, and the Army of the Deccan, under General Sir Thomas

Hislop, consisting of seven divisions, acting from different points.

The Peshwa had again been in trouble, and after the entirely purposeless murder of the Gaekwar's envoy, who was at Poona on a mission, had been compelled to agree to an arrangement which gave some promise of curbing his wayward character. Irked, however, by the trouble that he had brought on himself, he was watching for an opportunity to vent his hostility on the British. The Pindari trouble seemed to him an excellent opportunity to arouse the Mahratta chiefs, combined with all the Pindari hordes, against the British.

At this time the forces that a united combination might have brought into the field were extremely numerous, and were approximately as follows :—

Scindia . .	1,500 horse,	16,000 foot,	140 guns.
Holkar . .	20,000 ,,	8,000 ,,	107 ,,
Peshwa . .	28,000 ,,	14,000 ,,	37 ,,
Bhonsla . .	16,000 ,,	18,000 ,,	85 ,,
Amir Khan .	12,000 ,,	10,000 ,,	200 ,,
Pindaris . .	15,000 ,,	1,500 ,,	20 ,,

Such a potential and even probable enemy, with the vast power of the Pindaris to recruit their ranks with every bad character in India, who preferred plundering his neighbours to working for himself, was ample justification for the vast preparations of the Governor-General.

KIRKEE AND POONA

Matters were soon quickened by the action of Bajee Rao. Poona had been filling fast with levies of all descriptions, ostensibly to help us against the Pindaris. Their general behaviour became insolent and threatening, and various detached British officers were murdered. A battalion of the Bombay European regiment had been pushed up to support the subsidiary force cantoned at Dapuri near Kirkee. The Peshwa now demanded the withdrawal of the European battalion, and advanced on the 5th of November 1817 to attack the British force, which had withdrawn from its cantonment and was drawn up on a ridge at Kirkee, close to what is now the grand trunk road running through the present cantonment. The British under Colonel Burr was joined by Mr. Elphinstone, the Resident, who had with difficulty escaped from Poona. The Mahratta force numbered some 18,000 horse, 8000 foot, and 14 guns.

The British numbered some 2000 native troops with 800 Europeans. In addition to the Bombay

European regiment a detachment of the 65th Foot was present, with some native artillery, and five Bombay native infantry regiments, with one auxiliary battalion. This latter eventually formed what is now the 123rd Outram's Rifles, while the other battalions that still survive are the 102nd Grenadiers, and the 112th and 113th Infantry. The glory in this battle of Kirkee lay in the *audace, encore l'audace*; for the small force advanced against the huge hordes that had poured out of Poona over the Mutha river,

On the March.

65th Regiment of Bengal Native Infantry, 1840.

and swarmed round it on the plain between Ganeshkind and Bamburda. As the force advanced, the Mahratta horse swept round it, to the confusion of some of the native corps, who, however, quickly rallied. The good Atkins of the day led the charge, a cannon-ball struck down the Mahratta banner, a grape-shot killed the leader of horse, one Moro Dixit, and the huge force broke away from the field, to tell its fears to the Peshwa, praying to heaven from the gilt-topped temples of Parbutti Hill. Since a fine daring often brings its own reward, the British casualties were not severe. The Kirkee force was then left unmolested, and shortly after, on the 13th, the advanced portion of the 4th division arrived under General Smith and, forcing the ford near what is now the Bund at Poona, drove the enemy from the city to the hills beyond.

Seetabuldee and Nagpore

At Nagpore, the Bhonsla's capital, the Mahratta chief had been assembling his own forces, ostensibly to assist against the Pindaris, and the moment news came of the trouble at Poona and the Peshwa's outbreak, his troops at once became threatening. The British subsidiary force at Nagpore consisted of three troops of the 6th Bengal Cavalry (not the present 6th), the 1/20th and 1/24th Madras Infantry, and some details of artillery, with some local troops. The Bhonsla, as did most of the other chiefs, maintained a large force of Arabs, and these to the number of 3000, with huge bodies of horse, swarmed round the Residency. So threatening had been their attitude that the British moved out of their lines on the 15th of November and occupied the two small hills of Seetabuldee which overlooked the Residency, and entrenched themselves. All that night and the next day the Arabs and Mahrattas attacked the position, the Arabs being most daring in their attacks. The unfortunate troops had left their families in the lines, and heard the shrieks of the occupants, who were killed and ill-treated. Captain Fitzgerald made several desperate charges with the 6th Cavalry, in which young Hearsey was wounded and achieved great distinction, being long known as "The Hero of Seetabuldee." This officer, as General Sir John Bennet Hearsey, commanded the Dinapore division when Mangal Pandy, just before the Mutiny, shot his adjutant and thus shed the first blood in the great rising. The Seetabuldee main hill was definitely held, the smaller one was taken and retaken, though the enemy finally broke off the fight, not, however, before the British had lost 121 killed, of whom five were European officers, and 241 wounded, of whom 13 were European officers. In the period of strained relations, word had been sent calling up the 2nd division under General Doveton, and this force reached Nagpore on the 12th of December, and on the 16th attacked the enemy who, to the number of 21,000, were entrenched in villages and gardens near the city. After several hours' fighting they were in full flight, leaving 64 guns on the field. Five thousand Arabs and Hindustanis, however, threw themselves into the city, and it took several days of bombarding and attempted assaults before the garrison surrendered. The British losses at Nagpore were 141, chiefly from artillery fire. It is very noticeable in this war that the casualties were not nearly so heavy as in the earlier one. Lord Lake and General Wellesley had destroyed the trained infantry that each chief maintained. With the exception of the Arabs, who fought most courageously, and who were an object of immense dread to our native troops, the forces against us were chiefly masses of elusive irregular cavalry, who could not be destroyed in one pitched battle, and it took months of weary pursuit before they could be accounted for.

Of the troops that shared in the desperate defence of Seetabuldee, only the 61st Pioneers remain, then the 1/24th, but who had for a long time been the 1/1st. The troops who took part in the battle of Nagpore that are still on the Army

List are the 1/22nd Bengal Infantry, now the 6th Jats, and the present 61st, 62nd, 81st, 83rd, 86th, and 97th, and of course the ubiquitous Madras Sappers and Miners.

CORYGAUM

While the Bhonsla was adding his share to the confusion, and losing his throne thereby, General Smith and the troops at Poona were pursuing the Peshwa, who had retired to his chain of forts in the Western Ghats, from which every sort of opportunity existed for successful doubling. At the end of December, evading General Smith, he was again threatening Poona. Colonel Burr commanding there then called to his assistance the garrison of Sirur, which place lies between Poona and Ahmednagar. Captain Staunton in command marched with the 2/1st Grenadiers, now the 102nd Grenadiers, 2 guns of the Madras Artillery under Lieutenant Chisholm, and 250 Reformed Horse under Lieutenant Swanston. These latter were some partly organized horse recently in the Peshwa's service. On marching into the village of Corygaum they found the whole of the Peshwa's force encamped on a stream opposite the village. Twenty thousand horse with 8000 infantry, including 3000 of the dreaded Arabs, immediately advanced on this small force, which threw itself into such of the village enclosures as were not already in the possession of the enemy. By noon the British were closely invested and cut off from the water, and exposed to the most desperate attacks of the Arabs, and a heavy artillery fire. Till 9 P.M. that night the attacks continued, when at last the disappointed Arabs and Mahrattas drew off after suffering severe loss. In the fight almost all the European gunners were killed or wounded, and Lieutenant Chisholm's head was cut off and taken to the Peshwa. One of the guns was carried by the Arabs, and Lieutenant Pattinson, a gigantic subaltern of Grenadiers already mortally wounded, led his men to recapture the gun. This mortally wounded giant of six feet seven, in his dying effort, himself accounted for five Arabs, and exhorted the failing troops to renewed efforts. Assistant-Surgeons Wyngate and Wyllie led the men equally with the combatant officers, the former being killed later in the day by the enemy, who captured the courtyard in which he was lying wounded. Lieutenants Swanston and Conellan, who were lying severely wounded with him, were only rescued at the last moment. The losses of this determined band were more than heavy. Out of the 24 Europeans of the Madras Artillery 12 were killed and 8 wounded, while the Grenadiers lost 50 killed and 105 wounded, and the Reformed Horse had 96 casualties. Only Captain Staunton, who commanded, and two other officers were unhurt. A tall basalt column to this day stands to commemorate the gallantry of this small band, and the Grenadiers yearly keep festival on the anniversary.

At daylight next morning the Mahrattas, scared by the news of General Smith advancing to the rescue, made off and broke up.

MAHIDPORE

While the attacks on their subsidiary forces by the Peshwa and the Bhonsla had been taking place, with the troops that they had assembled ostensibly to help us against the Pindaris, the other divisions of the Army of the Deccan and the Grand Army had advanced into the area which contained the various strongholds of the commanders of the different Pindari *darras* or bands. These various hordes were driven from their fastnesses and gradually broken up. Sir

Thomas Hislop, commanding the Army of the Deccan, had crossed the Narbudda and advanced to Ujein, keeping, however, one eye on Holkar lest his forces, too, should play us false. Holkar himself was a lad, under the guardianship of Tulsi Bai, a mistress of the famous Jeswant Rao Holkar of the former wars. Tulsi Bai was in favour of peace with the British, whereon the war faction in the State chopped her head off and set their troops in motion. Sir Thomas Hislop then advanced towards them, negotiating with the Durbar as he went, with a view to the preservation of peace. Peace, however, was not to be, and on the 20th of December 1815, the British found that the Mahratta force was at Mahidpore, a few miles ahead, and consisted of some 5000 infantry with 100 guns and 30,000 horse. There were, however, many with that small British force of 5500 men who had fought a larger number of Mahrattas with even smaller numbers at Assaye, and knew the value of *l'audace*. So before day-break on the 21st Sir Thomas advanced with Sir John Malcolm, commanding a strong advanced guard. The enemy were as usual drawn up with a river on their front (the Sepra), one flank opposite the village of Mahidpore, the other on the river.

The details of the battle were as many of its forerunners. The infantry crossed the stream and attacked in the face of a long line of guns, followed by the cavalry and artillery, and the Mahratta horse broke away at once, though the infantry stood their ground, and the gunners died at their guns. The whole of the immense camp and treasure was captured, with supplies and munitions of all sorts. The British loss was as heavy as in some of the battles of the earlier war, though nothing like so serious as Assaye. It totalled 174 killed and 604 wounded. The troops engaged consisted of the flank companies of the Royal Scots, and the whole of the Madras European regiment, while the native troops all came from the Madras Army, and the Russell Brigade. The following corps that took part are the Madras Sappers and Miners, the 63rd, the 74th, the 87th, the 88th, the 91st, the 94th, and 95th (both of the Russell Brigade, which was later the Hyderabad contingent), and the 28th Light Cavalry. A pursuit was organized a few days later, and Holkar's Durbar concluded a treaty.

The Capture of the Peshwa and the Break up of the Pindaris

Scindia, it should have been explained, had been overawed by the advance of the Grand Army, and had not joined, or let his troops join, with the Pindaris. Holkar was now settled with, and little remained but the weary task of finishing up the operations, and completing the destruction of the Pindaris. It was to take, however, over a year more of pursuits and sieges. The mountains in the theatre of war were covered with inaccessible forts, while numerous strong walled towns and fortresses in the plains acted as continual havens of rest to the enemy. The pursuit of the Peshwa after the action at Corygaum was taken up on all sides in succession, and he was run up and down the country, as were the remnants of the commanders in South Africa. Bajee Rao himself finally surrendered to Sir John Malcolm in May 1818. The chase of Bajee Rao is still famous in the country-side, while the people say that the beat of the hoofs of his thousands of horse may still be heard o' nights. He was removed to Bithur and pensioned, dying there in 1854.

After this there still remained the Bhonsla and

the Pindari chief Chetu, with dozens of lesser bands. Numerous columns, reduced the mountain forts, while the mounted corps pursued the broken horse. Appa Sahib, the Bhonsla, eventually fled to the Punjab. Chetu Pindari, hunted and solitary, was killed by a tiger, and there only remained Aseergurh, which belonged to Scindia, but whose governor refused to obey his order to surrender. It had become the refuge of the desperate, and finally fell, after a siege and a loss of 323, to the British. The garrison surrendered a few days before the storm, and were almost entirely the Arab, Mekrani, and Sindi mercenaries from the State troops and Pindari bands. Among the many more important sieges in which the Arabs were also the principal garrisons, were Malegaon and Garhakotah. In the Southern Mahratta country the sieges of Belgaum and Sholapore were important. With the fall of Aseergurh the land had peace till the Mutiny once again stirred Arab and Pathan and free-lance to run riot over Central India, and a similar campaign to that against the Pindaris was necessary to free the land and hunt down Tantia Topee.

The big Mahratta States, as a result of this war, were once and for all confined to their legitimate territories and such conditions as suited us, and did not again dispute with the British the overlordship that they had tried to wrest from the Mogul.   The army of Scindia, it is true, did break out owing to domestic disturbances, and was destroyed in the short Gwalior campaign of 1843, and with it the last trace of the old French military pattern, except so far as a few traces endured in the Punjab.

To that belated medal " To the Army of India," already alluded to, were added the following clasps for this war : " Kirkee," " Poona," " Kirkee and Poona," " Seetabuldee," " Nagpore," " Seetabuldee and Nagpore," and " Maheidpoor."   It will have been noticed that the bulk of the heavier fighting fell to the Madras Army, which was still at its prime.   The Grand Army, though engaged in plenty of harassing work, was more immediately concerned with watching some of the larger States and preventing the Pindaris from breaking into the Doab and Bundelkhund.

After the war the military organization of the three armies was overhauled, and some uniformity of system introduced, with many improvements in enlistment and equipment, for which the experience of the Peninsula and recent wars in India was utilized.   These two prolonged wars are certainly noteworthy as the two greatest wars in which the army of John Company had been engaged, and also the hardest.   The employment of eleven divisions at once, besides many detachments, is striking proof of the large force which their responsibilities and dangers had enforced the Company to maintain. How the demands on them still further increased with their responsibilities in Afghanistan, Scinde, and the Punjab, has already been referred to, and the result that followed in its train, as many think inevitably, must now be described before the modern army that rose from the ashes of the old can be treated of.

CHAPTER III

THE hard-fought battles of the Sikh wars and the annexation of the Punjab bring us within a few years of the turning-point in the history of the Indian Army. It has been shown how that army grew from a force of doorkeepers and watchmen, to an army of 311,000 native soldiers, regular, irregular, and local. We have seen how at one time the remnants of the fighting forces of the free-lances and warring barons flocked to the British standard, and how the low-caste Hindu became an efficient soldier in the coast armies. Then gradually, if we may believe the diaries and the autobiographies of the old officers, there came what is spoken of as the "brahmanizing" of the native army. That is to say, as war became less constant, the consideration of other matters than securing the best fighting animal, actuated the authorities.   The race of adventurers began to die out, and the need for employing disbanded hostile soldiers became less pressing, while our officers came to know more of the better classes of the people.   It was perhaps thought desirable to get them into connection with the army.   At any rate, the desire became general to confine enlistment to high-class races, to whom certain other classes, that had made such good soldiers, were beneath contempt as fellow-men.   To get these men of social prejudice to serve, it was necessary to discontinue enlistments of the lower castes in the same corps. The army came to consist largely of the better castes, men who were chiefly the yeomen peasants of the country.   Now there can, of course, in many ways be no better stock than this for a soldiery, but in the East, long years of alien rule and constant invasion had reduced many of the peasantry of the South to a state of spirit that made them unsuited to military service.

In the eyes of many of the old officers the higher castes in Southern India were by no means the best soldiers, and generations of oppression, or years of peace, had deadened the habit of the sword.   In Bengal, however, the same tendency had different if not less harmful results.   The population of Behar and Oudh consisted of a manly and warlike peasantry of fine physique and martial appearance, and withal orderly and obedient. Gradually, the whole of the army in Bengal, with the various contingents and local corps dependent on it, and corps to which the Bengal officers were appointed, enlisted more and more of this convenient and suitable material.

In 1857, in Bengal alone, irrespective of contingents, locals, and military police, there were 137,000 regular troops, of whom close on 20,000 were cavalry. A very large number of these were Poorbeahs, as they were called, or men of the eastern provinces; in other words Rajputs and Brahman clans from Oudh. In the ranks of the regular army, men stood mixed up as chance might befall. There was no separating by class and clan into companies. The Bengal regiments were leavened with a considerable number of Muhammadans, and after the Sikh wars with some Sikhs.

These latter, by reason of their wild appearance, were not welcomed, and were only enlisted in deference to stringent orders of Government. In the lines, Hindu and Muhammadan, Sikh and Poorbeah were mixed up, so that each and all lost to some extent their racial prejudices, and became inspired with one common sentiment. When the trouble came, the Sikhs in the Bengal regiments, either infected with sympathy for the men of their corps or too isolated and distributed throughout the companies to dare assert their own feelings, joined in the Mutiny in the first instance, while their compatriots flocked to the British standards. At any rate, by 1857, the mass of the Bengal Army consisted of the same material, the soldierly and obedient Brahmans and Rajputs of Oudh and Behar, chiefly the former. The gradual regularizing of administration, the desire of the Court of Directors for information, the call for statistics and all the bureaucratic tendency of a vast government, militated against the discipline of the army. The power of commandants of corps had been reduced, petitions from sepoys to superior authority received attention, the bonds of discipline slackened. The vast increments to our dominions called for many Europeans to fill the various offices of government. It was economical to draw on regiments for officers for civil and semi-civil appointments. The regimental cadres were large, on the scale of the British service, viz. 1000 privates, 120 N.C.O.'s, 20 Native, and 24 British officers. It is true that some of the best corps were the irregulars, which had but three

British officers, but the irregular system especially developed the initiative and responsibility of the native officer. In the Line the British officer did most of the work; and though as many officers were not required in peace as for war, still, the process of selecting officers from corps, without filling up their places, resulted in many of the best men preferring employment in the interesting work of developing new provinces, to the humdrum routine of station life. The regiments of late years had therefore lost some of their best blood. The vast increase in the numbers of the native corps, without any counterbalancing increase in the Europeans, due to the vast new tracts to be held, has been already noticed. This, added to what has already been described, and the loss of prestige due to our disasters in Afghanistan, together with the unexpected severe casualties suffered by the troops in the Sikh wars, had gradually reduced the prestige and content that had appertained to military service.

Added to this was the fact that the permanent occupation of districts that had already been occupied as a temporary measure induced Government, whose financial position always affected their actions, to abolish the field - allowances usually granted to temporary garrisons in districts outside British India. This latter step was the signal for considerable show of insubordination. The 66th at Wazirabad showed such ill-feeling that the Commander-in-Chief, Sir Charles Napier, in the absence of the Governor-General on a sea voyage, ordered the immediate disbandment of the corps.

During the hundred years that had elapsed between the battle of Plassey and the Mutiny, many acts of mutiny of varying gravity had occurred, and usually over the question of pay and allowances. On two occasions had these mutinies been on the part of the British officers of the Company's Army. In 1764 the Bengal sepoys had mutinied for higher pay and gratuities, and only two years later the British officers in Bengal conspired, and ceased from duty on a question of *batta* (field-allowance), and this mutiny was only put down by the determination of Lord Clive. 1806 was specially remarkable for the mutiny at Vellore, which was far more serious than any of its predecessors. In its significance it might well have been regarded as a warning. At Vellore dwelt the pensioned family of Tippoo Sultan, the ousted ruler of Seringapatam, who had fallen in the final storming of the fortress. His family were removed and pensioned in favour of the Hindu dynasty, that he himself, or rather his father Hyder Ali, had supplanted. It is probable that the discontent of a dispossessed family and their entourage had resulted in an endeavour to tamper with the fidelity of the native troops. An unthinking order regarding the wearing of caste-marks in uniform, and the pattern of turban to be worn, gave light to a conflagration that had been preparing for some time. The native troops of the Madras Army garrisoning Vellore fell on the British troops also in the fort, and killed many before they recovered from the surprise. The remnant were barely able to defend themselves with considerable further loss, till relieved at the last gasp by Colonel Rollo Gillespie of the 19th Light Dragoons at the head of an advanced detachment of his regiment. This mutiny was found to have widespread ramifications.

In 1809 the British officers of the Madras Army rebelled, owing to certain real or imaginary grievances, and had to be suppressed with a heavy hand. Again, in 1824, some Bengal infantry battalions, under orders to march towards Arracan, refused and were severely handled for their pains. After the occupation of Scinde and the annexation of the

Punjab, the troubles and insubordination regarding the *batta* came to be acute, as already described.

For some time occasional warnings had been uttered against the native army, organized, as has already been described, in a vast imitation of a European Line. To many of the statesmen who had served in India, Sir Henry Lawrence and others, the huge possibilities underlying the pre-ponderance of this vast mercenary force over its European counterweight had the obsession of a nightmare. The warning utterances, how-ever, had not sufficient weight, or were given under circumstances that deprived them of their value, such as Sir Charles Napier's criticisms, and the letters of Colonel Jacob criticising the discip-line, organization, and efficiency of the Bengal Army. The Bombay Army of those days had a practical efficiency far ahead of the Bengal troops. In Herbert Edwardes' book, *A Year on the Punjab Frontier*, he tells (himself a Bengal officer) of his seeing the Bombay brigade join the Bengal troops under General Whish, before the fortress of Mooltan. He relates how struck he was with the practical equipment of the troops, which included water-bottles and haversacks, and with their military alertness, so superior to that of the

Bengal battalions, but which he attributed to the —to his ideas—dangerous custom of promoting non-commissioned officers and native officers for their military efficiency apart from their length of service. Safety apparently in the Bengal Army had been provided for by assuring that no man should come to any status till he was past the age of activity. The inscriptions on the cross alongside the long trench graves at Chillianwalla, as already related in the preceding chapter, are a witness to the age of the native officers, and in the Company's service the same system prevailed for British officers. In the old graveyard at Saugor, sometime the headquarters of a division, may be seen the grave of a general officer who died in " command of the Narbudda division of the army " at over eighty years of age. It is hard to expect the characteristics of the soldier at even three-score years and ten.

It is interesting to note how the army, modelled on the safe system of incompetence, was the one to blow up so soon after this comparison had been drawn.

Lord Dalhousie, as may be seen from his private letters that have only recently seen the light, was very fully aware of the volcano on which he sat, and long proposed to himself to try to reform it; but constant pressure and growth of territory were to prevent him from putting his hand to the difficult ploughing.

So, despite warning and premonitions and head-shakings, and a universal feeling that however well the army was dressed and the belts pipeclayed there was something rotten, 1857 found us with the army as described, with peace on the surface and a canker below. The literature that has described the Mutiny and discussed its causes is perhaps only beaten in its volume by that of the American War of Secession, and its various phases need only be lightly passed over here. Though, however, Lord Dalhousie had recognized that the native army was out of all proportion, wrong in its constitution, and deficient in European counter-weight, still he himself confessed in these same letters of his, written in this case during the Mutiny, that he had never foreseen anything in the way of a general mutiny and massacre, and that with a hundred years of fidelity and more behind it, there was ample reason for some confidence. On the other hand, the private accounts of the Sikh wars constantly allude to the accepted belief that the Sikhs had been tampering with the Poorbeahs, and that the reluctance of some corps to advance was due to this.

Be that as it may, 1857 opened in considerable peace and contentment; the Ganges Canal had not long been open, and its hundreds of miles of ample water had brought much promise to many thousands of peasants. Oudh had been annexed with unexpected simplicity. A new Governor-General found little to harass him. Then came the outbreak at Barrackpore, whence the general name of the mutineer was derived. Early in January of that year came the first news of the greased cartridge incident. It had flown all over India with extraordinary speed. In the end of February, the 19th at Berhampore in Bengal refused to take the ordinary exercising blank cartridge. After threats and persuasions they took them in sullenness and flew to arms that night. The officer commanding the station marched down the native artillery and cavalry to the 19th lines, and the men were finally persuaded to replace their arms, without recourse to force, which probably the other troops would have refused to use.

At Barrackpore, the headquarters of a division, to which the 19th had now been ordered to march, were the 34th Bengal Native Infantry, who had

openly avowed their sympathy with the 19th.   In
the evening of the 29th of March, the guard of
the 34th were reported in an excited
state, and one, Mangal Pandy, shot
the adjutant who rode up, and the
European sergeant-major who came
up also and called on the guard to
protect their officer.   The guard
then struck them with the butts of
their rifles.   The divisional commander, General Hearsey, famous as
a leader of sepoys, and known when
a lad as the " Hero of Seetabuldee,"
coming up at this juncture, rode
straight at Mangal Pandy, who then
tried to shoot himself.

1st Gurkha Regiment,
1861.

A Soldier out of
Uniform.

The disturbance was then quelled,
and the General at once promoted
a naik who had come to the rescue of his adjutant.
It is interesting to know that the General received
a wigging for doing so from the Military Department.   Some show of promptness in the way of
punishment did follow, however, for Mangal Pandy
and the native officer in charge of the guard were
shot before a month had elapsed.   By this time
the state of the army was the absorbing interest.

The classes at the musketry schools had spread the tale of the greased cartridge all over India. Officers were discussing the affair with their native officers, but no apprehension of a large mutiny was entertained. All over the country, officers professed the most profound confidence in their own regiments. This, curiously enough, continued up to the last stages of the Mutiny, and however much neighbouring corps might misconduct themselves, officers had full confidence in theirs. This attitude, so much derided by outsiders at the time, was perhaps one of the most remarkable tributes to the innate faculties that enable British officers to lead alien troops. When you have lived with soldiers for years, led them to victory, and heard all their troubles, who will believe that they are about to rise? Who would expect, for instance, the 35th Native Infantry, the portion of the " Illustrious Garrison " who, emulating Clive's sepoys at Arcot, had given up their rations to the Europeans of the 13th Foot in Jellalabad, and feasted these same comrades at parting, would mutiny? This same spirit of trust between British officers and their men exists to-day, and only so long as it exists will the native army be a fighting force. With the great shadow behind, however, it cannot be carried to the blind extreme that so honoured the sepoy officers of 1857.

It is agreed by all who have studied the subject, that the greased cartridges were a fortunate incident, from the plotters' point of view, which merely gave head to a movement that had had many different centres for many years.   The British rule, with its immense weight, its different ethics and standards, and its craving for administration, had become unpopular, for many reasons that need not here be reviewed. To the dread of many of the princes and the hatred of the priests, was added the long-felt disgust of all those classes, to whom the free-booting services and conditions prior to the Pindari war had brought so congenial a livelihood.   It is always hard for the Baron and his men-at-arms to settle down to a reign of peace and simple agriculture. The greased cartridges, the admitted thoughtlessness of a military department, were a god-sent incident to act on the arrogance of a spoilt but reasonably contented army of mixed religions, and it was used to its full by the extremely capable heads who were pulling the strings of the move-ment.   After this occurrence rumour followed rumour, and discontent and uncertainty appeared at many stations, with unexplained fires chiefly in officers' quarters. Then at Meerut came the well-known test parade of the 3rd Cavalry to receive their old ammunition, under the eyes of the large European garrison. The refusal of 85 men to take the cartridges, their trial by a court-martial of native officers, their heavy sentences, the manacling parade of the whole garrison to see the fetters riveted on the mutineers, and the outbreak on the evening of the next day, Sunday, the 11th of May, are well-known matters of history. As the Europeans were parading for evening service at Meerut the native troops broke into open revolt, murdering every Christian man, woman, and child that they came across. The stupor of surprise that allowed the mutineers to escape need not be described here; the fact was patent that, in the words of the *Red Pamphlet*, "THE BENGAL ARMY HAD REVOLTED." How those mutineers made off, unpursued, to the old Imperial city of Delhi, and were joined by the troops there, and the rabble that surrounded the mock court of the pensioned descendant of the Great Mogul, to likewise slay all the English they could lay hands on, is equally a twice-told tale. In a few weeks, from Patna to the Peshawar valley, the Army of Bengal was in open mutiny, and half the Barons in the country-side with it.

The mutineers, largely Hindu soldiers from Oudh, proclaimed the re-incarnation of the Mogul Empire, compelling the aged pantaloon Bahadur Shah, son of blind Shah Alam, to pose as the Emperor of India.   Then as the tally of regiments mutinied in all the main cantonments, they flocked to the great centre at Delhi and the old Imperial name.

Sir Henry Lawrence in Oudh had held havoc in hand for several weeks, till the mutiny of the large garrison at Lucknow and the Oudh Irregular Force, with the attraction of the Europeans at bay, formed a second focus for rebellion.

The mutinous regiments, under command of their native officers, marched to Delhi, to Lucknow, or to Cawnpore, with their British colours flying, wearing their British war medals, with their bands playing British airs.   The British on the ridge before Delhi could often hear the mutineer bands playing the airs their officers had taught them, before the Emperor's palace.   The anomalies of the Mutiny were many.   In some regiments the officers were murdered with every possible atrocity. In others great pains were taken to conduct them within reach of a place of safety.   Some officers received offers to assume command and lead them to the service of the Padishah, after the manner of the European free - lances, whose adventures were still a topic in the land. Here we read of the *subadar-major* taking an affectionate leave of his commanding officer, but demanding his epaulettes or his full-dress coatee as the price of safe - conduct. *Psychologie des foules*, in all its forms, was to be experienced. Careful study of the inner history of the many mutinies of 1857 almost unfailingly elicits the conclusion that the great bulk of the army did not mean to mutiny and massacre its officers. The clever cliques in each regiment, to whom the ferment had been entrusted, knew their game thoroughly.

The soldiery, in many ways simple and confiding as children, were fed on every possible rumour. One day the bulk of the regiment or the older native officers, with tears in their eyes, would protest their loyalty to their colonel and comrade of fifty years. The next morning he and his officers would be dead in the rising sun.

It has been urged as an instance of the inconsistency and perfidy of the Asiatic that it always seemed that the best-beloved officers were the first to fall, as a regiment rushed to its bells of arms, and devoted officers hurried into the lines to calm their men's excitement.   But does not this rather tend to show how well the men managing the rising knew their business ?   In every native regiment there are always two or three officers whose disposition has gained them the confidence and affection of the men in an exceptional degree. These officers hold a regiment, as it were, in the palms of their hands.   Once they were out of the way, the ship would be without a rudder.   It was no hard matter for the desperadoes, usually the *pahlwans* or wrestling clique, to shoot these officers before the rising clamour had got beyond control.

Then, while the well-affected stood aghast, the leaven would spread, the desire for blood rise . . . a few more shots, and the regiment would stand so committed that all must stand or fall together. Such, no doubt, was the inner history of most of the mutinies, at times appalling in their atrocities, at times astonishing in their mildness.   Corps mutinied unexpectedly, without regard to time and reason.   A few, like the 50th Infantry at Nagode, mutinied even after the fall of Delhi must have proclaimed the hopelessness of their cause.

How, or when, or at what moment the mutinous desire seized a regiment, no one could tell.   In the words of an old mutineer, '*hawa laga*' . . . a wind blew . . ., exactly as a crowd knows not who first kicks the man who is down.

At any rate, the fact was soon patent that the whole, with a few exceptions, of the great Bengal Army had disappeared in this whirlwind, taking with it most of its kindred contingents and affiliated irregulars. Those corps that did remain true to their salt, mostly owed their escape to circumstances and a location that removed them from a participation in the feelings of the rest of the army, or debarred them from the opportunity of displaying their disaffection. The irregulars in some cases failed almost as hopelessly, though not so universally as the regulars, and the local corps were little better. There were, however, a few honourable exceptions, notably the 31st N.I. at Saugor, who, when the rest of the garrison mutinied, remained staunch, and operated vigorously against the rebels, while the 65th and 70th N.I., who had volunteered for China and were serving there while their comrades were in mutiny, may fairly be given the benefit of the doubt. At the end of the Mutiny, fifteen battalions of regular infantry out of over seventy regiments of the Bengal Line, and none of the regular cavalry, remained on the Army List. So departed the glory of the Bengal Army.

The Madras Army, however, had been little touched by the storm, for reasons many and various. Difference in race, difference in system, and perhaps the embarrassing custom whereby a sepoy was allowed to have all his family with him in cantonments, and on the march, helped to discount all tendency to rebel. In the still smaller Bombay Army sedition was not so universally absent, for it was not to be expected that the Mahratta would miss so golden an opportunity for intrigue. In the Southern Mahratta country, where there had been a war in 1844, with confiscations and annexations, there was plenty of tinder to help kindle a flame, which, however, never really assumed large proportions. The Madras and Bombay Armies, as well as the Hyderabad Contingent, took an active part in suppressing mutiny and rebellion in various parts of India, notably in Central India.

During the progress of the Mutiny in Hindustan proper, the stern and resolute spirit manifest in the Punjab overawed the Bengal regiments. The garrison at the capital, Lahore, of which Mian Meer was the cantonment, was disarmed by a *coup de main*, while the populace marvelled Rebellion in the Peshawar valley was stamped out ruthlessly, and only in one or two stations did mutiny raise its head with success. This decision appealed to all the hardy men of the north, who were waiting to see how the cat meant to jump. The Punjab Irregular Force eagerly responded to the call to march south. The disarming of the Bengal Line regiments in Peshawar, and the punishment of those who tried to mutiny, captivated the mind of the border tribesmen, who, at first merely watching, now eagerly flocked to serve.

The Irregular Force, led by the Guides, marched south. Every sort of irregular horse and tribal levy was formed, some to keep themselves in order, others for Hindustan.

The motives that brought the Punjab and the Border to our aid, were no doubt mixed ones. Some content with our administration, some liking for English ways seen at their best in the cold of the Northern winters, some memories of the hard hitting of Sobraon, of Chillianwalla, and Gujarat, a dislike of the Poorbeah, our abetting instrument in conquering them . . . all had, no doubt, their place. Probably first, however, among the motives of those who enlisted in the new corps was the thought of the wealth of Hindustan. To this day, if you talk to a veteran of the siege of Delhi, he will tell you perfunctorily of this skirmish and that fight, and show you on the ridge where So-and-so fell, but his eyes will glisten and his old heart warm, when he tells you of the Chandni Chowkh, the jewellers' street of Delhi.   The old soldier who went to the Baillie Guard, the relief and capture of Lucknow, that is to say, will talk as much of the loot he brought away as of the fighting.   According to him, the return of the Guides to the frontier was a sight to see, and was talked of in the Punjab for many a day after.   Beautiful ladies transferred their affections to the men of the north, and rode in carts behind the baggage of the corps, and with them wealth that was the envy of every soldier of fortune in the country-side.

A Khyberi of the Queen's Own Corps of Guides, 1853.

However, whatever the mixture of primary motives actuating the irregular soldiery that helped the British Line to reconquer India, they followed their gallant leaders unflinchingly, and with loyal affection, and were more than true to the salt they ate.   The corps which they went to form, now remain as some of the *élite* of the army, and have served since, with as much distinction as that which they won in '57, in many more of the Sirkar's wars.

The fidelity of the Frontier, or as it was then called, Irregular Force of the Punjab, the alacrity of the Punjabi and frontiersman to serve, added to the steady loyalty of most of the Bombay and Madras corps, together enabled us to reconquer Hindustan. It must also be remembered that though chiefs and Barons and their followers turned against us, and villagers hastened to rob and to loot, the great mass of the people had no desire to see the last of us. The army before Delhi lacked neither supplies nor transport, nor the most faithful domestic service, from even the earliest days.

Among the many irregular corps that came to fame in '57, in addition to the existing corps of the army, were Hodson's Horse, Wale's Horse, Lind's Horse, Cureton's Multanis, the Mahratta Horse, the Sikh Irregular Cavalry (three corps), the Delhi Pioneers, the Sikh Volunteer Infantry (raised from the Sikhs of corps that had revolted), with eighteen regiments of Punjab Infantry, and local levies innumerable. When the last embers of the Mutiny had died out, and the last gang of hopeless Poorbeahs and outlaws had surrendered or fallen in action, the task of rebuilding a new army on the ashes of the famous red-coated line of the Honourable East India Company, was no light task. The Company hardly knew what its stock of irregular troops was, for they had been raised as emergency demanded and opportunity offered, on authority which, even if existing at one time in writing, was often not forthcoming afterwards. Opinions innumerable existed as to what was to be done. The whole subject was much complicated by the transfer of India to the Crown, and the formation of a Royal instead of a Company's Army. How that task was carried out, and what the measures then taken have ultimately developed into, it is the principal object of this book to illustrate and explain.

CHAPTER IV

WITH the raising of the irregular regiments in the
Punjab, commenced the Indian Army of to-day.
When, a year or so after the Mutiny, the proclamation transferring India to the Crown was
read before the large force then garrisoning
Peshawar, it is on record that on the left of
a long line of troops, clad in the loose khaki
clothing that is now so familiar, stood a corps
that a twelvemonth had made as extinct in Upper
India as the dodo. There stood, in its scarlet
coatees, its shakos and white cross-belts, a surviving Bengal regular battalion, that had alone,
of the original Peshawar garrison, escaped dis-
armament and avoided mutiny. The influence
and character of its officers must have been far
beyond the ordinary, to have kept that regiment
still standing under arms.

From the discussions that ensued on the close of the campaigns that succeeded the revolt, it had been decided to organize the whole of the native force on what has already been described as the irregular system. The existing nucleus and model was the now famous Punjab Irregular Force. In the first hasty numbering of the newly raised infantry in the Punjab, they had been organized on the same status as the Irregular Force, numbered consecutively after the existing corps, and assumed to be, as that force was in peace time, under the control of the Punjab Government and not of the Commander-in-Chief. The eighteen new battalions had been numbered from 7 to 24. It was now decided to renumber the loyal remnant of the old army from 1 onwards, according to seniority, both infantry and cavalry, and to add on to these the new corps, renumbering them also in succession.

The actual numbering between 1860 and 1861 was altered several times in the Bengal Army, owing to change of policy and plans. At first the Gurkha regiments, which had been extra battalions, were numbered with the new Line. Already the original Nasiri battalion had been taken into the Line as the 66th, when the original

66th mutinied in the 'fifties over the *batta* trouble, and it was first decided to include them all. Then came orders to keep the Gurkhas as a separate Line of their own.

The final numbering of the new Bengal Army was as follows (under G.G.O., 990 of 29.10.61) :—

1st Bengal N. Infantry.			The old 21st.
2nd " "			" 31st (of Saugor staunchness).
3rd " "			" 32nd.
4th " "			" 33rd.
5th " "			" 42nd.
6th " "			" 43rd.
7th " "			" 47th.
8th " "			" 59th.
9th " "			" 63rd.
10th " "			" 65th.
11th " "			" 70th.
12th " "			" Regiment of Khelat-i-Ghilzai.
13th " "			" Shekhawati Battalion.
14th (Sikhs) "			" Regiment of Ferozepore.
15th (Sikhs) "			" Regiment of Ludhiana.
16th " "			" Regiment of Lucknow.
17th " "			" Loyal Poorbeah Regiment.
18th " "			" Alipore Regiment (Calcutta Militia).

This closes, with a few exceptions, the list of the Bengal Infantry corps that escaped the cataclysm.

The 12th had been raised as a battalion of Shah Soojah's Contingent at the time of our first Afghan venture, and after its famous defence of Khelat-i-Ghilzai it was brought into the Company's service as an extra battalion. The 13th, 14th, and 15th had been local battalions, the two latter of Sikhs, raised in the Cis Sutlej States, before the Mutiny. The 16th is a famous corps, in that it is composed of the loyal detachments who stuck to their officers when the Lucknow garrison mutinied, and who formed a very much larger portion of the effective fighting strength of the garrison than is usually remembered. It was remembered at the time and after, but at half a century's lapse we are apt to forget some of those who kept the flag flying during those weary, scorching months. The 17th was formed from similar detachments from various regiments, while the 18th were an old local corps who maintained their honour under trying circumstances.

The new 19th to the 32nd Native Infantry were 14 of the 18 regiments of Punjab Infantry raised in '57-'58, and temporarily numbered in succession with the six regiments of Punjab Infantry in the Irregular Force; while the 33rd to the 40th were various local corps raised as

"Levies" during the Mutiny. The 41st, it is interesting to note, were the 1st Infantry of the Gwalior Contingent, and the 42nd, 43rd, and 44th were the old Assam and Sylhet Light Infantry battalions. Three Line regiments that had survived the Mutiny, the 4th, 58th, and 73rd, were disbanded, as well as several local battalions. The Gurkhas were renumbered as follows : the 66th or original Nasiri Battalion became the 1st Gurkhas ; the second Nasiri Battalion, which had broken out into semi-mutiny at Jutogh and scared half Simla into the jungles, before it went down to help keep the Delhi-Punjab road open, was subsequently disbanded. They had been raised to take the place of the original battalion taken into the Line as the 66th already referred to. The Sirmoor Battalion became the 2nd Gurkhas, the Kumaon Battalion became the 3rd Gurkhas, the Extra Gurkha Battalion became the 4th Gurkhas, and the Hazara Battalion became the 5th Gurkhas, remaining as before part of the Punjab Irregular

British Officer,
Madras Horse Artillery,
1845.

Force.   A few years later Rattray's Sikhs, raised as a military police battalion after the Sonthal rebellion of 1856, was mustered into the Line as the 45th Sikhs.   The highest number of the Bengal Line remained at 45 for many years.   The cavalry in Bengal were similarly renumbered.   All the regular cavalry and several of the irregular corps had mutinied or been disarmed, or otherwise come under suspicion.   In 1861, orders appeared renumbering the whole of the cavalry, some being old irregular corps, others local horse of recent standing.   Before the Mutiny there were eighteen regiments of irregular cavalry.   Of these eight were finally retained and renumbered, according to their own original seniority, under the same G.G.O. of 1861 as the Infantry, viz. :—

1st Bengal Cavalry, formerly the 1st Irregulars.

2nd	,,	,,	2nd	,,
3rd	,,	,,	4th	,,
5th	,,	,,	7th	,,
6th	,,	,,	8th	,,
7th	,,	,,	17th	,,
8th	,,	,,	18th	,,

Then to these were added the famous regiments of horse raised for the suppression of the Mutiny:—

9th Bengal Cavalry, formerly 1st Hodson's Horse.
10th   „   „   2nd   „   „
11th   „   „   Wale's Horse (later Probyn's Horse).
12th   „   „   2nd Sikh Irregular Cavalry.
13th   „   „   4th Sikh Irregular Cavalry.
14th   „   „   Murray's Jāt Horse.
15th   „   „   Cureton's Multanis.
16th   „   „   Rohilkand Horse.
17th   „   „   Robart's Horse.
18th   „   „   2nd Mahratta Horse.
19th   „   „   Fane's Horse.

Fane's Horse was originally raised after the Mutiny from volunteers from other corps, for the expedition to China.

The Punjab Irregular Force, which was not under the control of the Commander-in-Chief, was left at its original strength of 5 cavalry regiments, 4 battalions of Sikh infantry (the old Sikh locals of the Jullundur Doab), and 5 battalions of Punjab Infantry. Their light field batteries and mountain trains were finally fixed at four, and converted to mountain batteries, with one garrison battery. The Madras and Bombay Armies were not renumbered, as mutiny had made no gaps in the former and but one or two in the latter. Certain corps raised and especially developed during the long hunt for Tantia Topee, and the marauding bands into which the embers of mutiny had turned, remained under the orders of the Government of India, and were not brought into the Line at that time, such as the Central India Horse, the Erinpura Irregular Force, the Deoli Irregulars, etc. Some of these irregular corps comprised both horse and foot, and at one time guns.

The whole of the European artillery and the corps of engineers were transferred to the Royal corps under special conditions. The mutiny of all the native Bengal artillery, and other weighty considerations, had decided the Government to have no native field artillery in future. All the native artillery was therefore gradually disbanded. The only exceptions to this rule were the four mountain batteries in the Punjab Irregular Force (which force was called the Punjab Frontier Force in 1865), and two native batteries in Bombay. These Nos. 1 and 2 companies *Golandaz*, originally used to garrison Aden and man the Jacobabad mountain train in turn, eventually became Nos. 1 and 2 Bombay Mountain Batteries, and later 5 and 6 (Bombay) Mountain Batteries. Another exception were the four field batteries of the Hyderabad Contingent. The whole of this contingent had done excellent service in 1857, and was retained intact. In future, with these exceptions, the artillery service in India was to be found by batteries and companies of the Royal Artillery. A sapper and miner corps was retained in each Presidential Army, officered from the Royal Engineers.

The new corps had all been organized on the so-called irregular system, which has already been described, and which in its early days meant that the command of companies and squadrons was in the hands of the native officers, and that only the command, second in command, and regimental staff, were in the hands of British officers. This had the merit of cheapness, and was well suited to the immediate post-Mutiny military conditions. The term irregular was, of course, an ill-chosen one; it was only irregular in that it differed from the old sealed pattern organization, that had tried to follow the regimental constitution of Europe.

The question was also taken up of applying this system to the Madras and Bombay Armies, after the moot question had been decided as to whether or no there should be one Indian army or three armies. In that day there was no Suez Canal, and Europe, for troop-transport, was far away. The mass of opinion was in favour of water-tight

SMITHS
CASE-HARDED GLASS
S.1

A.C.LOVETT

compartments, by which it was meant that three different armies, organized and constituted differently, were a great safeguard against general mutiny; and the staunchness of the coast armies in the recent trouble did certainly bear out the argument.

Gradually the whole, however, of these two armies was organized on the same system as regards officers.   The whole of the cavalry, except four regiments of Madras Light Cavalry, was organized on the silladar system which obtains to this day.   Its whole principle is that Government pay so much per head, and the regiment finds everything except firearms.   In the original days of silladar cavalry, it meant that the trooper received this amount and found himself in everything.   In these days, when a regiment is expected to have itself equipped in a uniform way, it means that the men are required to enlist with a certain amount of money towards the purchase of their horse, and the regimental commander administers their pay so as to make it gradually cover

British Officer,
3rd Madras Light
Cavalry, 1845.

all the various articles of equipment they require as well as to feed the horse. For this sum the regiment also provides its baggage animals. The administration, therefore, of a silladar cavalry regiment requires immense business capacity on the part of a commanding officer. The system has produced some splendid light cavalry, and has appealed to the best material in the country. It has also been admirably suited to irregular and frontier war, and the need for a sudden well-equipped move when the tribes are rising. It is not a very easy system to maintain in a war of any size or duration, while the continual rise in price of horses, food, and equipments always tends to make the silladar rates of pay a little behind the times.

The Madras Line practically retained its old numbers, as did the regiments and battalions of Bombay, the other coast army. The Company's European battalions of the three armies were transferred to the Crown, and as regiments of the Line have much added to their already ample laurels. Three regiments of European Light Cavalry, raised for the Company during the Mutiny, and known to fame as the "Dumpies," by reason of the small and gin-fed recruits that were at first forthcoming, were transferred also as the

19th, 20th, and 21st Hussars.   At the time of this transfer, occurred that instance of mismanagement, that while once and for all clinching the argument against a local European force, was both sad and dangerous. The "White Mutiny," as it was called, was a widespread and determined opposition on the part of the Company's Europeans, led in some places by the artillery, to the orders transferring them to the Crown. The Crown had been advised that the terms of the men's engagement included service under the Crown, and that an act of transfer was completely legal. The men thought otherwise, and considered that they should be allowed a discharge or a bounty. The crisis that arose was a source of great anxiety just at the close of the Mutiny, and was by no means creditable to the troops. Before it was quelled, one unfortunate had to be publicly executed. The Government then decided to modify their attitude, and thousands of men took their discharge home to re-enlist in the Queen's troops on arrival. It was one of those unfortunate occurrences of which the inner history is hard to know.

Allusion has been made to the vexed discussion as to whether or no the European troops in India should be local. This waged very acutely, and it is interesting to read in the reviews of the time, that it was held by well-informed men that if there were no local European service the native army would deteriorate to the level of a " Black Militia." So unkindly does print and time treat the prophets.

The transfer of the large cadre of officers of the Indian Army, to a force serving under entirely different conditions (for purchase still obtained in the Royal Army), produced many anomalies and much discontent. The mutiny of about half the army with large cadres of officers, and its replacement with fewer corps with small cadres of officers, meant that very many were without employment. As they had definite rights as regards periods of service, they had to remain on if they wished, and throughout India were to be found officers of the old cadres doing general duty in cantonments or commanding isolated forts and sanatoria.

With the reforming of the Army of Bengal, another controversial question came into prominence, viz. that of class regiments versus class companies. That is to say, whether regiments should consist of only one race, or whether different races should be kept in different companies in the same regiments. It will be remembered that, in the old army, men stood by chance in the ranks, Hindu and Musalman, Poorbeah and Punjabi, cheek by jowl. The object aimed at in the new construction was, to some extent, to put the races into water-tight compartments, while at the same time developing their feeling of clan emulation and martial characteristics to the full. There was much to be said for both of the proposed systems. The balance of argument was on the class company. To put the analogy into English terms, it was as though a battalion should have so many English, and so many Scotch or Irish companies, or so many Catholic and so many Protestant companies, or should be entirely of one race.

Accordingly, the majority of the new regiments became class-company ones, and only a few Sikh and Gurkha corps remained entirely homogeneous. In the older armies the old constitution was to a great extent retained, but the number of Poorbeahs (literally men of the Eastern provinces), the race which had mutinied, was strictly limited. This system of class companies gradually led to a very close study of the clans and races of India, which will be discussed and described in the next two chapters.

Before, however, the new Crown Army had

settled down after the struggle and re-organization, it was once more called on to perform its Imperial rôle. The war in China that had been patched up in 1857, once more broke out, and a strong force from India was hurried off from the campaigning ground of the Mutiny to the celestial capital, in co-operation with a French force in the advance on Pekin in 1860. The force was drawn from all the armies, but some six of the newly raised irregular regiments from the Punjab took part. Even during the Mutiny itself the usual frontier operations were taking place in the Peshawar district and on the Assam frontier, while in 1860 an expedition was sent against the Mahsud Waziris. In 1864-65 operations against Bhootan were necessary, and in the autumn of 1864 we were forced into the operations in the Peshawar valley, which brought in their train the rising of the whole of the tribes in Swat, and the desperate fighting in the Ambeyla Pass. The desperate fighting connected with the repeated capture and recapture of the Crag piquet is a famous incident of the campaign. In 1867-68 the expedition to Abyssinia was undertaken, in which the Bombay Army took a considerable part, with a strong Bengal brigade. Lord Napier of Magdala's march from

Zula on the Red Sea to Magdala, with its wonderful arrangements for food and transport over most difficult country, will always be remembered. 1868 also saw an expedition against the raiding tribes of the Black Mountain and several other minor operations.

1878 saw us once more involved in Afghan affairs, owing to the Amir's reception of a Russian mission and refusal to receive a British one under Sir Neville Chamberlain. The war that followed was a long and costly one, and had two distinct phases; one, the advance towards Kabul on the north, and to Kandahar in the south, with the treaty of Gundamuk and the succession of Yakub Khan to the throne of his father Sher Ali; and the second, the advance to Kabul after the murder of the British agent Sir Louis Cavagnari and his escort there. The war is memorable for the famous actions at Ali Musjid, the Peiwar Kotal, and Charasiab, and the heavy fighting round Kabul; later on came Ahmed Khel, the disastrous defeat of Maiwand, and Lord Roberts' march from Kabul to Kandahar, with the successful battle under the walls of that city. The conclusion of the campaign left us with a more convenient and logical frontier, and especially with the possession of British

Baluchistan. The Bengal Army and Frontier Force formed the bulk of the Kabul Army; and the Bombay Army, the Kandahar Army, while several units from the Madras Army were moved up on to the lines of communication.

Just before this war, an Indian force had been sent to Malta in readiness to join a British force to act if need be in the Russo-Turkish War. In 1882, a strong Indian contingent joined Sir Garnet Wolseley in Egypt, and shared in the decisive fight at Tel-el-Kebir, eighty years after the original brigade under Sir David Baird had sailed to join the British there. In 1885 Indian troops again went towards Egypt, this time to the Soudan; while the same year the situation brought on the Third Burmese War, in which representative corps of the whole three armies took part, and which ended in the annexation of Upper Burma.

Daffadar.
13th Duke of Connaught Lancers.
Watson's Horse,
1885.

During the Afghan and Burmese wars it had become evident that several corps in all three armies were recruited from material that was no

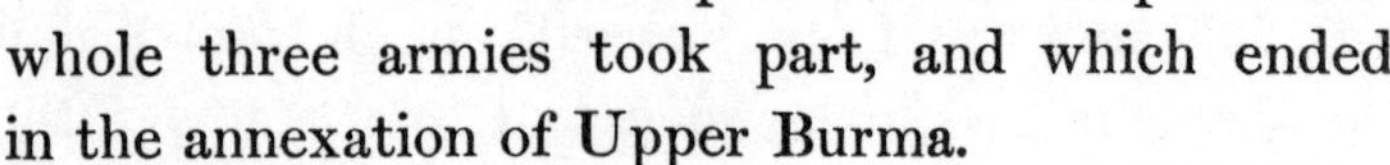

longer suited to the trying climate and arduous conditions of the modern theatres of war. Several regiments of the Bombay and Madras Armies were reconstituted with Baluch, Pathan, and Punjabi soldiers in the ranks. The Madras regiments thus altered were located in Burma, the Baluch and Pathan regiments in Scinde and Baluchistan. In the Bengal Army, more battalions of Gurkhas were raised, and also a corps enlisted from a kindred hill-race in Garhwal. The Madras Army had made immense efforts, too, to improve its quality by tapping certain likely races within its own territorial limits; and Moplahs, an uncouth race from the western coasts, with hillmen from the uplands of Coorg, were enlisted into class corps. Experience eventually led, however, to the corps being broken up.

The immense expenditure incurred in the prosecution of the war in Afghanistan led to the reduction of several corps of cavalry and infantry in 1882. In 1885, however, the necessity for war preparation that was the sequel to the Penjdeh incident, had seen half the Indian Army mobilized to take the field in Central Asia, and the demand for troops showed the shortsightedness of the '82 reductions. Most of the reduced corps were restored to the establishment, under an improved class constitution. The few blank numbers that a scrutiny of the Indian Army List will reveal as still vacant, are mostly a relic of the '82 reductions.

During the 'eighties, in addition to the overseas expeditions recorded, there were several small frontier operations, including the Sikkim expedition, which brought us regularly into touch with Thibet. 1888 to 1892 brought two expeditions to the Black Mountain, one to the Samana, and one among the mountains of Hunza Nagar on the borders of the Pamirs, as well as several minor expeditions in the Chin and Kachin hills of Upper Burma. So that some portion of the Indian Army was always under arms.

In 1894, the fierce fanatical attack on the escort to the Boundary Commission in Waziristan, forced on us an expedition against the Mahzud Waziris for the third time, and brought us into closer relations with a more than usually faithless and fascinating class of tribesman. In 1895, the British Agent at Gilgit had occasion to visit Chitral, on the occurrence of one of the usual cataclysms in the reigning dynasty, and was attacked and shut up in Chitral fort by Pathans from neighbouring States. This resulted in the Chitral Relief

Expedition, with its fight at the Malakand Pass, *en route* to Chitral, from the Peshawar Valley, and Kelly's sensational march from Gilgit in the north. In 1897, events of many kinds, the encroachment of civilization, salt dues, the joy of possessing better arms, and the drum ecclesiastic rolled after the triumph of Turk over Greek, combined to produce such a crop of simultaneous frontier risings as we had never before seen. First Waziristan blazed off, in the treacherous attack on a small escort at Maizar. Then in the north, the tribes of Swat threw themselves for days in succession against the British garrisons at the Malakand and Chakdara, for the glory of God and the Prophet. While the force that had relieved these posts was inflicting punishment on the offending tribes, the Mohmands further south threw themselves across our borders, and were defeated at Shubkadr. Before the troops could gather to repel the Mohmands the fiery cross had sped, the tribes of Miranzai and the Samana were in a blaze, and as troops were hastened there, the Afridis of Tirah must needs attack the Khyber posts and close the road. By this time the situation had become most difficult, and the Government all at once had some four different campaigns on hand, of more than usual dimensions. From the north to the south of India, troops of all kinds and classes had to be put in motion, and operations lasted for practically ten months. Some of the events, notably the storming of the Dargai heights on the road to the Afridi Tirah, are well known. The close of the campaigns found us for the time being with considerably increased garrisons, till in Lord Curzon's viceroyalty the policy of local levies, on the old Black Watch principle, was extended, and the troops themselves gradually withdrawn.

During the period covered by these campaigns, many changes had been in progress within the army itself. In 1886, the Punjab Frontier Force was transferred from the direct control of the Government of India, to the ordinary control of the Commander-in-Chief in India; while in 1895 came the great change which had been long foreshadowed, viz. the abolition of the Presidential Armies, as separate armies under separate governments, with separate Commanders-in-Chief. After the Mutiny this question was much discussed, but at that time railways were hardly even in their infancy in India. Central control was almost impossible, while the water-tight compartment seemed the immediate lesson to be derived from the Mutiny. As India had modernized, and the railway system had overcome the difficulty of the vast distances, it was evident that three Commanders-in-Chief were an anachronism ; and at last, after much discussion, the Bengal Army was split up into two commands, and these with the Madras and Bombay Armies were constituted into four Lieutenant-Generals' commands, with a Commander-in-Chief over all. The numbering of the various units of the army was, however, for the time, left to stand, with the many anomalies that such an arrangement presented. There were in the army, liable to serve side by side, both in peace and war, and often actually during the latter, the 1st Bengal Infantry, the 1st Bombay Infantry, the 1st Madras Infantry, the 1st Gurkhas, the 1st Infantry Hyderabad Contingent, the 1st Punjab Infantry, the 1st Sikhs, the 1st Burma Infantry, the 1st Baluchis, and almost as many 1st cavalries, etc. It was not till Lord Kitchener's period of command that this big question of renumbering could be successfully tackled. The abolition of the armies in 1895, however, was the forerunner of the general numbering.

Then during this period, the recruitment of class and clan and the recruit-yielding capacity of the various races began to be most carefully studied, and as one class after another came to show the results of years of peace, the search for a better soldier - bearing stratum became more stringent. Orders appeared from time to time, altering the constitution of regiments as experience and change of times proved the need, till gradually the present arrangements, which it is now proposed to describe, were evolved.

CHAPTER V

THE MILITARY RACES OF INDIA

IT is one of the essential differences between the East and the West, that in the East, with certain exceptions, only certain clans and classes can bear arms; the others have not the physical courage necessary for the warrior. In Europe, as we know, every able-bodied man, given food and arms, is a fighting man of some sort, some better, some worse, but still as capable of bearing arms as any other of his nationality. In the East, or certainly in India, this is not so. The people of Bengal, even those with the most-cultivated brain, the trading classes, the artizan classes, and the outcaste tribes, are men to whom the threat of violence is the last word. At the bottom of all power and law, disguise it never so carefully, lies the will of the hand to keep the head. Presumably the great conquest of India away back in the mists of time, by the Aryan race, and the subjection of the original inhabitants, is at the bottom of this. Only certain races were permitted to bear arms, and in course of time only certain races remained fit to bear arms. Conquest, pure and simple, with cruel repression, is responsible for it in some places, such as in Bengal and Kashmir. It is extraordinary that the well-born race of the upper classes in Bengal should be hopeless poltroons, while it is absurd that the great, merry, powerful Kashmiri should have not an ounce of physical courage in his constitution, but it is so. Nor are appearances of any use as a criterion. Some of the most manly-looking people in India are in this respect the most despicable.

The existence of this condition, therefore, much complicates the whole question of enlistment in India. It renders any form of levy *en masse* impossible, or any form of Militia service, while it emphatically forbids the English system, whereby the well-to-do pay for the lower orders to do their fighting for them. In India itself certain classes alone do the soldiering and kindred service. These are, roughly, in central and northern India the yeoman peasant, the grazier, and the land-owner. Very good classes, too, as every one can see, and in India there is no exodus from the land to the crowded city.   The peasant in India, that is to say, the yeoman peasant, is a well-born man, distinct from the mere helot of low birth who in some parts helps on the land.

Now the people by tribes from whom we take soldiers in India itself are as follows :—

    (1) The ancient Aryan races, who invaded India in prehistoric times, viz. Rajput (lit. sons of princes) and Brahman, who for practical purposes may be divided into two distinct classes, those of Hindustan and those of the Punjab.

    (2) The races of Jāts or Jăts, and Gūjars.

    (3) The Pathans and the Moguls of India.

Then from outside the limits of India :—

    (4) The Pathan and Afghan of the frontier hills.

    (5) The Gurkha.

Then we have a further division which is by religion, and also another by country.

For instance, we have the Sikhs, who are largely that portion of the Jăt race which embraced the calvinistic reformed Hindu teaching of the Sikh *gurus*, and who live in that part of Upper India known as the Punjab, the land of the five rivers.

Then we have the Muhammadans of the Punjab, who are of many mixed races, but who largely consist of Rajput tribes converted to

Islam at various times in the past. They describe themselves as Rajput rather than Muhammadan.

The Muhammadans of India are either the descendants of conquering or serving foreigners of that faith, or of converts. In whichever category they may claim descent, they will generally be of mixed origin by now, and those who claim Pathan and Mogul descent will have lost the characteristics of their race, and even their features, for it is rare to see a sign in these days of the Tartar origin of the Moguls.

Then, again, in the Southern Plateau we have the Deccan, of which the people are largely Mahrattas or Marathi-speaking, and, mixed with them, Muhammadans of varied origin.

For the purposes of describing the military tribes and castes it will be as well to do so by countries and provinces with certain exceptions. The gradual raising of the military standard by the change of times and terrain, and the enervating effect on Asiatics of a few generations of peace, have already been referred to. It has resulted in a gradual enlistment of an increasing number of men of the northern races, whom a cold winter, and a lesser period of the enjoyment of peace, have for the present preserved from military deterioration.

It will be reasonable, therefore, to commence with the races of the north, viz. of the Punjab and the North-West Frontier.

The Military Classes of the Punjab

The Sikhs.—It is not correct to speak of the Sikhs as a race ; they are, properly speaking, a numerous religious sect, which, starting as a persecuted set of reformers, became a powerful sect embracing many of all the Hindu tribes and races of the Punjab. The first *guru* or spiritual teacher of the new faith was Baba Nanak, born in 1469, near Lahore. Brought up within the influence of the teaching of a one and only God as conceived in Islam, he taught a reformed or puritan Hinduism, in which simplicity, kindliness, purity, and brotherhood were among the leading principles. Stimulated by repression and persecution, the sect grew and flourished. Nine *gurus* succeeded father Nanak; the tenth *guru*, the famous Govind, succeeding his father at the age of fifteen, on the former's suffering death and torture at the hands of the Mogul. In the hands of the tenth *guru* the religious and peaceful community was changed into a powerful military sect, that constantly obtained fresh recruits and became the champion of the Hindu inhabitants against the Musalman. The faith spread to most of the Hindu tribes of the Punjab, more especially to the vast cultivating race, the Jăts, which to this day is spread over the whole of Upper India.

H.H. Raja Sir Hira Singh Bahadur of Nahba, Hon. Colonel 14th Sikhs.

Because the Jăts form, perhaps, two-thirds of the Sikhs, the term Sikh (which means disciple) is largely associated with the *Jăts.* These same Jăts, however, number many hundreds of thousands who embraced the hostile creed of Islam, while in Rajputana and about Delhi and south of it are numerous Hindus of the same descent who call themselves *Jāts* (*q.v.*). To the generic title of Sikh or disciple, the warlike Govind added the affix Singh or lion, originally the affix of men of Rajput race.

A Sikh is baptized into his sect and not born into it, so that no man is a Sikh till he has taken the *pāhŭl,* that is to say, till he has been baptized.

Sikhism is an austere faith, demanding some simplicity and rigour of life from its adherents. So much is this so, that for many years there has been a tendency for young men to avoid the *pāhŭl* and grow up as ordinary Hindus, for whom life has few irksome restrictions.   But as the value of the Sikh as the simple, faithful soldier, has lain in his adherence to the simple tenets and hardy life of his forebears, no non-baptized Sikh is admitted into a regiment of the Indian Army.   So careful are regiments in this matter, and so much are regiments the home of the old martial and simple Sikh principles, that it has been said, not without some shadow of truth, that it is the British officer who has kept Sikhism up to its old standard.   The creed of Govind is thus described :—

Emerging from his retirement he preached the *Khalsa*, the faith of the pure, the elect, and the liberated.   He openly attacked all distinctions of caste, and insisted on the equality of all who would join him.   Resuscitating the old baptismal rite of the Sikhs, he proclaimed it as the *pāhŭl* or gate, by which all might enter the fraternity, while he gave to its members the *pershad* or communion as a sacrament of union in which the four orders of Hindu society should eat from the same dish ; . . . the higher orders murmured . . . but the lower orders rejoiced at the new dispensation and flocked in numbers to his standard. . . . He gave them the outward signs of their faith, in the unshorn hair, the short drawers, and the blue dress.   He marked the military nature of their calling, by the title of *Singh* or lion, by the wearing of steel, and by the initiation by sprinkling water with a two-edged dagger, and he gave them a feeling of personal superiority in their abstinence from the unclean tobacco.[1]

But while Nanak substituted holiness of life for vain ceremonies, Govind Singh demanded brave deeds and zealous devotion to the cause as the proof of faith. . . . Religious fervour was entirely eclipsed by military zeal, and thus for the second time in history a religion became a political power, and for the first time in India a nation arose, embracing all races, all classes, and all grades of society, and banded them together in face of a foreign foe.[2]

Such in brief is Sikhism and its history. The *Jăt* Sikh forming the bulk of the fraternity are those who have served us most, and who probably make the best soldiers. The *Jăt* is a peasant farmer before anything else, however. In spite of the military tenets of his faith, his sayings are all of the plough, and a plough is the first toy of the Sikh's son. The *Khatris,* who have embraced Sikhism, form largely the business class, and have been enlisted in small numbers for their brains . . . the *Jăt* being proverbially thick in the uptake, . . . and have served with distinction. The *Lobana,* the hereditary carrying class, have always

1 *Sikhs.*   Bingley.
2 Sir Denzil Ibbetson, *Ethnography of the Punjab.*

done well as soldiers, though not very largely enlisted. The greater demands of the army on the hardier races of the north have, however, caused the recruiter to closely examine the yield in Sikhs of other classes, with the result that certain regiments enlist no *Jăt* Sikhs, but have been successful in some of the smaller and humbler Sikh communities. For instance, *Sanis* or gardeners, *Kumboh* Sikhs, a cultivating race of putative foreign origin, of whom some are Sikhs, the artificer classes, have all been swept into the military net, which only their Sikhism has made possible.

The *Jăt* race, from whom so many Sikhs were made, is described farther on under Jāt and Gūjar, but must be referred to here. There is much discussion as to their origin, but it seems probable that they are in reality of a Scythian race, with whom some identify the Jātii of history and the Magyars and gypsies of Eastern Europe. To what extent, and when, they mingled with the Aryan race, and to what extent the distinction between them and the Aryans is social, it is impossible to tell. The Scythian tribes undoubtedly adopted Buddhism soon after their arrival, and later Hinduism. All *Jăts* are cultivators, and the name has become almost the name of an occupation. The inhabitants of the Indus Valley when that river leaves the mountains are largely Muhammadan Jăts. (See later " Jāts and Gūjars.")

One more Sikh community needs description, since they form so faithful a portion of the Sikh soldiery, and these are the *Mazbi* Sikhs who serve in the Sikh Pioneer regiments. The term *Mazbi* means faithful, and was applied to the sweepers of outcaste tribe who brought back the crucified body of Teg Bahadur, the second successor to Guru Govind. Their descendants of outcaste tribe, and probably those outcastes whom they converted to Sikhism, now have the title. They served under Ranjit Singh, and were formed into a pioneer regiment for service before Delhi, since when their courage and general good qualities have made them famous for the work of the military pioneer.

The military services of the Sikhs in our service are well known. The Sikh regiments, whether those raised just before the Mutiny, such as the 14th or 15th Sikhs, the regiments of Ferozepore and Ludhiana, or the 35th and 45th (originally a military police corps), are equally famous, as are those regiments that enlist class squadrons and companies of Sikhs, and the regiments of Pioneers.

Their military reputation, so far as our service is concerned, largely dates from the Mutiny, when the Sikhs flocked to our standards. Since those days, the Punjabi generally, but especially the Sikh, has become a world-wide adventurer. In addition to enlisting in every sort of military or police body that will take him, in Africa, China, or the East generally, he is to be found also as watchman in many private firms. High pay is what attracts him, and wealth to spend on his land when he returns home. These attractions, and the devastation of plague in the last few years, have made the Sikh recruiting-market tight, and there is little doubt that we have, if anything, over-recruited from this nationality. The large number of men they furnish, *vide* the next chapter, their importance as a population, and the latent possibilities underlying the tenets of their creed, all make their description at some length desirable. In appearance they are well known: tall, well-knit men, with their long hair pulled up under their headdress, their beards and whiskers neatly curled up close to the face, and their military bearing all stamp the man, even to those with only a bowing acquaintance with Hindustan. As a fighting man, his slow wit and dogged courage give him many of the characteristics of the British soldier at his best.

The Muhammadan of the Punjab

The Muhammadans of the Punjab, exclusive of the Pathan, who will be described later, consist for the most part of men of the various Hindu tribes who have at one time or other accepted Islam. The better classes inhabit more or less their own districts and are largely Rajput, and describe themselves as Rajput. They keep themselves separate by clans, and in some cases, such as the Chibs, count kin in some sort with those of the tribe who remained Hindu. There are, of course, tens of thousands of Muhammadans of the lesser castes and classes of no particular descent scattered about in every sort of occupation. It is the zemindar, the land-owning peasant, that the reputable mass of the population consists of, and who claim to be of Rajput stock and clan. Among them are certain clans and tribes who claim a foreign origin, and to have entered with one of the invasions, and, having occupied the lands of others, founded a barony and brought the owners to subjection. Among the latter are a well-known military clan, the Gukkhars, while among the

Rajput clans are the Bhattis, Suttis, Chibs, Janjuas, Tiwanas, etc.   The Awans, again, are another large tribe whose origin is uncertain, but from whom we draw many soldiers.   The Muhammadan tribes of the Punjab furnish many excellent soldiers, and since all the world over men are prone to exalt their station, so is a man seeking service given to say that he belongs to a better tribe than his own. The greatest care is taken to see that men do not represent themselves to be what they are not. Regiments enlist men of certain tribes and endeavour to keep to men of those tribes, so that in the companies that exist, tribal pride and emulation and even tribal discipline and public opinion may be stimulated.   All arms of the service enlist the Rajput Muhammadan, some tribes, such as the Tiwanas, only going to the cavalry.   The best of the Musalman tribes come from the Salt Range, that tumbled pile of sand and limestone crag that lies between the Jhelum and the Indus.

Allusion has already been made to the Jăts and the numberless tribes of this race that have embraced Islam.   They are so numerous that they have not received any very close study, and it is doubtful if the term *jăt* does more than imply cultivator in many cases, and the ethnography of the so-called Jăt tribes of the Muhammadan religion will bear far more study. Jăt Muhammadans, however, are not at present largely enlisted. Each class regiment and class company regiment has the tribes and clans whom it is to enlist either laid down by superior authority, or by regimental rule, and this is strictly observed. Great precautions are taken to ensure that the men really are what they profess to be, and their statements as to birth and tribe, etc., are sent to the civil authorities to be verified and corroborated, should the guarantee of the Indian officers in the regiment or other reliable evidence be not forthcoming in the corps. It must always be remembered that in India, military service is a source of much honour and prestige, so that pretenders will often try to pass themselves off as better born than they are. The essential difference, then, between the voluntarily enlisted army of the United Kingdom, and the voluntarily enlisted army of India, is at once evident. The English soldier does not always come to the ranks because it is the most honourable career he knows. The Indian soldier does.

The foregoing describes for the most part the fighting races of the Punjab other than the Dogras.

There are members of the great Brahman race scattered all over India, and those in the Punjab have imbibed the hardy habits that the climate has induced. A few are enlisted from the agricultural and land-owning clans, and make good soldiers. The various plates showing Sikhs and Muhammadan groups of the Punjabi regiments, illustrate the different physiognomy of the tribes and races, and also their national fashion of growing hair and beard, as well as the characteristic fashion of tying the pugaree, which in itself serves to distinguish race to the instructed observer.

The Dogra.—The Dogra is among the most valued of all the soldier races of Northern India. The name is really geographical and not racial. Dogras are people who come from the hills between the Punjab and Kashmir, and are the old Aryan Hindu stock and affiliated races who peopled the bulk of India. They are Brahmans, Rajputs, Jăts, and the like, who refused the Koran and the Prophet when many of the other Rajputs succumbed, and who later kept clear of the Sikh movement. Their situation in the foot-hills of the Himalaya, off the trampled path of the legions, may account for their retaining the religion and habits of the Aryan race. Certain of their related tribes, such as the Chibs, have in part, however, accepted Islam, and, when living in the Dogra country, are admittedly entitled to be styled Dogras, though in common parlance that term is applied to the Hindus of the outer hills, and more especially to the Rajput tribes.

Their good behaviour, courtly manners, high courage, and physical endurance, make the Dogra a valued soldier by all who know him. His enlistment is, however, only come to be widely undertaken during the last twenty-five years, and as a body they have not had the opportunity for acquiring fame that has presented itself to some of the other races. They have, however, invariably acquitted themselves with distinction. Three class Dogra regiments exist, the 37th, 38th, and 41st, while numerous regiments take one or more Dogra companies, and the cavalry Dogra squadrons. The higher class of Rajput is the more favoured, but those who will not themselves set hand to plough are as blue-blooded and as penniless as ever a Laird of Cockpen. The best clans are perhaps to be found in the cavalry. The Indian officer of the 12th Cavalry in one of the illustrations is a Dogra of a Rajput tribe. Another plate shows Dogras of Rajput and other tribes in the class regiments,

37th, 38th, and 41st Dogras, and a Dogra of the 31st Punjabis, which regiment is one of the many that has a class company of that race. Dogras come from the Dogra State of Jammu, the predominant State in the feudatory of Jammu and Kashmir (whose ruler is a Dogra Rajput of the Jamwal clan); from the British district of Kangra in the outer Himalaya, a part of the Punjab province; and from the foot-hills and submontane tracts between Jammu and Kangra. The State of Jammu and Kashmir maintains a considerable force of Imperial Service troops (*v.* Chapter VII.), who are chiefly Dogras, and who came to great distinction in the Defence of Chitral, Kelly's march to Chitral from Gilgit, and in actions with the Kohistanis near Chilas.

Pathans.—We now come to the great Pathan race, which is so inextricably bound up with the history of India, of whom many are now settlers in India, devoid of almost all their racial character-istics. Others live immediately within our North-West Frontier, while the bulk either occupy the unadministered hills between our administrative border and the treaty Afghan frontier, or dwell in Afghanistan itself.

It has been the fashion for all Afghans and Pathans for the last five hundred years to claim for themselves a common descent, and that descent a Jewish one. The Afghan proper, that is to say, the Durani clans, call themselves the Ben-i-Israel, the Children of Israel, and the legendary ancestor is one Kais, the chief of the descendants of a Jewish settlement in the Mountains of Ghor which lie north-west of Kandahar, and which to this day have never been visited by Europeans. To one of the three sons of Kais, all Afghan and Pathan tribes trace their origin, and cling to the Jewish legend. Kais was said to be 37th in descent from Saul, and lived in the days of the Prophet. There are settlements of professing Jews in Bokhara who preserve what may be an original legend, that they are the descendants of Reubenites, Gadites, and half of Manasseh, carried away to Central Asia by Tiglath-Pileser.[1] Be this as it may, the Afghans hold strongly by their Jewish origin, and their names, Jacob and Joseph and Isaac and Abraham and the like, do not belie the tale.

It is, however, pretty certain that a great many of the Pathan tribes do not belong to the real

---

[1] *The Kingdom of Afghanistan.* Tate.

M. Ahmed Singh
A C LOVETT

GUARD ROOM
553
A.C.LOVETT

Afghan stock, but are some Rajput tribes of the mountains who accepted Islam, and gradually assumed relationship with the Afghan confederacy, or were allowed the privilege of doing so in return for faithful service.   Again, the numberless invasions that swept into India by the Khyber, the Tochi, the Gomal, and the Sangarh passes, have perhaps left in their wake colonies that ejected, or mingled and assumed relationship with older tribes.

Whatever, therefore, may be the pretensions of all the tribes claiming Afghan descent to be of the true blood, the fact remains that the mountain life, cold climate, difficulties of livelihood, and community of religion, have produced peoples that resemble each other in their main attributes, without, however, the least homogeneity as a nation. Our venture to Kabul in 1838, to restore the dethroned king, Shah Soojah, to the throne of his fathers, as a British ally, first brought us into touch with the Afghans of Afghanistan and the independent republican tribes between Afghanistan and the Indus.   Our annexation of the Punjab brought our border and our administration into close relation with them.   Previous to this, however, the Afghan connection with India, dating from the days of

Afghan rulers and adventurers, and always kept up in some form, had brought many Afghans into the ranks of our irregular horse from the time of Lake and Wellesley onward.

Their systematic enlistment dates from the early days of the Punjab Frontier Force, but it was not till the Mutiny that it was at all regularized. The Pathan tribes are organized into many entirely distinct clans, claiming only the common Jewish, or perhaps some more recent ancestor. The clans have many subdivisions, and every clan and every sub-clan, and almost every family, has a feud, smouldering or active, which at times breaks out into raids in force, at times finds vent in the mere moonlighting murder of the Emerald Isle. Hardy, active, alert, and inured to war, are these clansmen of the Afghan hills, endued with considerable courage when well led, and capable of much *élan.* To the best type of Englishman their open, irresponsible manner and delight in all exercise and sport, with their constant high spirits, appeal greatly, and certain types of Englishmen appeal greatly to them also. When in the British ranks all blood feuds are closed, by custom as much as by discipline ; and a man may be stalking his right-hand man in the ranks, with knife and martini rifle, the moment furlough is open and they are across the border. Over the border 'tis border law, an eye for an eye and a tooth for a tooth, and the hand must keep the head, so that the young tribesman has his natural combatant faculties sharpened from the day he is weaned.

In addition to the clans beyond the administrative border, there are several wholly and some in part within the British line ; some, those who already dwelt within the Peshawar Valley, when an Afghan province ; others whose hills have for one reason or another gradually come within the administration, or who had come within the Sikh provinces.

All Pathans speak *Pukhtu* or *Pushtu*, as the hard and soft dialects of the language are called. *Pukhtu* is probably derived from the old Zend language written in the Persian character with many Arabic and Persian words. The Pathans or Pakhtŭns are the people who speak *Pukhtu* ; and since Herodotus speaks of the Pactydae who inhabited the Khyber, it is thought that the language and the folk who originally spoke it may have given a name to all who afterwards may have adopted it.

The Pathans who are enlisted in the Indian Army come for the most part either from within the British border, or between the administered border and the Afghan frontier. A few, however, notably in the Guides and the 124th and 126th Baluchistan regiments, come from Afghanistan itself. Great among the Pathan clans are the numerous collection of the Yusufzai, or the sons of Joseph. They live within the Peshawar Valley, or the hills bordering on it, and in the mountains towards Chitral, as well as in Buner, in Swat, and round the Malakand. They also dwell in the hills east of the Indus in the Hazara district, in what was for many years famous as a fighting-ground, viz. the Black Mountain. Their clans are many, and they make excellent soldiers, serving especially in the Guides. Between the Children of Joseph and the Khyber Pass, come the Mohmands and Utman Khel, who serve in our army, and always are prepared to fight us. South of the Mohmands come the Afridis, through whose hills the Khyber itself passes, and who are responsible for its safety and draw blackmail therefor, as many other highland clans before them in other lands. The Afridis are probably a Rajput or at any rate an Aryan tribe, though they have been fitted out with an ancestry of the Jewish community of Ghor. They are intensely republican or, more accurately, democratic, at times even paying no heed to their counsels of elders, every man a law unto himself. They serve in our army more than any other class, and are famous as good soldiers, and, of course, excel as skirmishers. Several thousand are in our ranks, and during the Tirah War (Tirah being the Afridi hills), when they too had been drawn into the wave of fanaticism on the border, the tribal representatives, who came to discuss terms of peace, usually wore British medals earned in our service.

The Afridi has less Jewish features than many of the Pathans, and some of them, with close-cropped fair hair and blue eyes, have a distinctly European appearance. It is curious, too, that on the border, Pathans of beautiful regular features are to be seen, especially among the lads, so that it is not incredible that the traces of the Greek soldier may still be visible.

Subadar-Major, 20th Brownlow's Punjabis. Kambar Khel (Afridi).

Between the Afridi Tirah, in the valley north of the Samana Range, are the Orakzai clans, who also give us soldiers.

South again of the Afridi within our border, are the Khattak Hills, from which comes another widely enlisted tribe, the Khattaks, who also lay claim to the Afghan Jewish descent. They have now been within our borders so long, that they have lost some of the less-desirable characteristics of their wilder neighbours, and make most courageous and reliable soldiers. Closely allied to them are the Bangash in Miranzai. South again of them, beyond the Bangash, up the road from Kohat into Afghanistan, comes the Kurram Valley, partly inhabited by a Shiah tribe known as the Turis. These only enlist into the local militia, but as such have obtained a considerable military reputation. They lay claim to the usual Afghan descent, but are thought to be of different origin.

Farther down the border between the Kurram and Baluchistan comes the tumbled mass of hills known as Waziristan, inhabited by what are now known as the Mahsud clans, the Darwesh Khel, and other Wazir clans. They give us immense trouble, but make remarkably fine soldiers, especially when, as in the case of the Irish, they serve away from their own land. The foregoing are the main clans from whom we take soldiery, who speak the Pushtu, and about whom and whose hills so much is heard from time to time. The clans are all, with the exception perhaps of the Afridis, intensely fanatical when stirred by the roll of the drum ecclesiastic. The majority profess a most unenlightened form of Sunni-ism, the orthodox form of Islam, but certain groups of clans, such as the Turis, the Bangash, and others, are Shiahs, and as such, heretics, and, except in war with the unbeliever, obnoxious to the orthodox.

The great race of Afghanistan proper is the Duranis, from Zemindawar and Ghor, and a few of them come to our ranks, especially the cavalry. There are, however, a considerable number of Duranis settled within British India near Multan and in the Derajat on the Indus. They are ordinary British subjects, but have maintained their ancient valour, and serve in such regiments as the 15th Cavalry (Cureton's Multanis), the 21st Cavalry (Punjab Frontier Force), and in the Baluch Horse. The Nawab Abdulla, head of the Alizai Section, is honorary native commandant of the 15th, and many of his family are serving or have served in the regiment. His portrait shows a type of a specially fine class of men, always ready to support us so long as we are true to ourselves.

Mention should also be made of the Hazaras, who are not Afghans, except in so far as they come from Afghanistan. They are a Tartar race and are much the same people as the original Moguls and Tartar hordes who overran China and Europe, and who as Moguls conquered India. Their language is the old Persian of Afghanistan and India. They are enlisted in the Baluchistan regiments, and a few years ago, an entire regiment, the 106th Hazara Pioneers, was raised from them, at a time when, owing to trouble with the Amir, many of them had migrated to British territory. They have for many years flocked to India to work as navvies, and make splendid pioneers as well as extremely smart soldiers.

Men of Pathan descent are to be found all over India, among the soldier settlers from old invasions. Until, indeed, the final extension of British rule to the Afghan border, the wild Afghan and Pathan clansmen have habitually sought their fortune in Hindustan, for the hills breed many and feed few.

The Baluchis

The Baluchis or Beloochis are a Muhammadan hill-race of probably Arab descent, who entered into their present abode from Persia and the Persian Gulf. They occupy a portion of what is now called Baluchistan.   In the hills, they have distinct tribal organization like the Pathans, except that they acknowledge implicitly the authority of their tribal chiefs.   Many Baluchis of broken tribes are scattered about the Indus Valley as landowners and cultivators.   The tribal Baluch of the hills is averse from military service except in local levies, but the broken tribe Baluch of the plains enlists freely.   The 127th, 129th, and 130th Infantry are known as Baluchi regiments, but owing to the reluctance of the Baluch of the hills to serve, have but few companies of this race.

RAJPUTS AND BRAHMANS

The history of the Hindu religion and the Aryan race in India is one with which all are familiar.   How, back in the mist of ages, the great Aryan race overflowed, or migrated, from the press of others, from the crucible of the human race in Central Asia, down through the passes of Afghanistan to the plains of Hindustan. How, after many generations of war between the original inhabitants, the whole or almost the whole of India owned their sway. How, a few centuries before the Christian era, a prince of the blood, named Gautama or Buddha, founded the reformed religion or rather philosophy known as Buddhism, which spread for some centuries over the land and into Thibet and China, only to lapse back in India, in the course of time, to Hinduism and Brahmanism. The main story, too, of Aryan evolution, so far as it is revealed to us through the many centuries that have elapsed, is common history. The Aryan invaders gradually broke up into three great divisions, the Kshattryas or soldiers, the Brahmans or priestly class, and the Vaisiyas or traders, merchants, cultivators, and the like. The Kshattryas, from being the followers and no doubt the clansmen of the princely leaders, gradually called themselves Rajputs, or the sons of the rulers. The Brahmans soon increased far beyond the power of their priestly craft to bring them bread, and took to cultivation ; and all three classes spread over the length and breadth of the land from Swat in the north to the hills on the fringe of the Himalaya, and to the plains of the south and the west.

Rajputs and Brahmans are still to be found all over India. The Rajputs in the Punjab have been described already, where, bearing the brunt of the wave of Islamic invasion, after desperate struggles they were compelled to accept the Prophet, but remain Rajput, which is the name of a race and not of a religion.

We have seen that they are to be found as the leading races in the Dogra hills, and also in Nepal, and shall find them far west in the Deccan. In India, however, especially in so far as recruiting is concerned, the term Rajput is usually understood to mean Rajputs of Rajputana and Delhi, usually spoken of as Western Rajputs, and Rajputs of Oudh or Eastern Rajputs. The chief centre of Rajput power finally came to be in the country of the Ganges and its tributaries, with Kanouj and Adjudya as the capitals. The wave of Islamic invasion, however, broke these kingdoms, and drove the Rajput centres to the edge of the Bikanir desert. The Rajput principalities, then formed in what is now Rajputana, held their own to a greater or less extent against the Musalman, and were finally admitted into alliance with the Mogul Empire. The Rajputs of Oudh took to agriculture, and, their tribal power broken, for many generations served as mercenaries in the Muhammadan armies. The Rajputs of Rajputana maintained their feudal system and held aloof from actual agriculture. Both classes have preserved many of their military traits, those of Rajputana being famous as horse soldiers and those of Oudh as footmen. The Rajput and Brahman of Oudh unfortunately formed the bulk of the army that mutinied, and lost their place in the army from henceforth. The few old regiments still enlist them, and of late years the principle of class and clan regiments has been extended to them, and has been carefully followed with far-reaching results.

The Rajputs are traditionally divided into three great branches, the Lunar race, the Solar race, and the Agnicular or fire clans, the latter being supposed to be Scythic clans admitted into the Rajput circle for political reasons. In fact there is no doubt that many of the aboriginal chiefs were endowed with Rajput ancestors exactly on the same principle as the Heralds' College will find ancestors of renown for parvenu families. The three Rajput races are subdivided into thirty-six recognized and so-called royal clans, which are to be found in various parts of the country independent of religion.

The Brahman race is roughly divided into the Gaur and Dravira divisions, with many clans in each.   The former are generally found north and the latter south of the Vindhya Mountains.   The military qualities of the Rajputs of Rajputana are famous in history and saga.   The military services of the Rajputs and Brahmans of Oudh in the service of the Company in the pre-Mutiny days are equally famous.   Since the Mutiny, Rajput and Brahman corps have taken part in minor wars with distinction.

The 2nd, 4th, 7th, 8th, 11th, and 16th regiments of infantry are Rajputs of Oudh and Delhi ; the 13th are Rajputs of Rajputana ; while several other regiments, infantry and cavalry, enlist Rajput companies and squadrons both Eastern and Western Rajputs.   The 1st and 3rd Infantry enlist Brahmans only.   The pride of race in both Rajput and Brahman is intense ; the former, especially the Rajput of Rajputana, being especially proud of the military history of his forebears.

The Jāts and Gūjars

The Jāt or Jăt race has already been referred to as one of the distinct races which are to be found under different religious banners in different parts of India.   As Jăts, those of them who form the bulk of the Sikh community have been already discussed as well as those who range under the crescent in the Punjab. The Jāts, Getae or Jātii of history, were a Scythian race who from Bactria have entered India by way of Southern Afghanistan and Scinde. Originally, it is believed, embracing Buddhism, they eventually joined the Brahmanical revival, and some of their leaders were admitted to the status of Rajputs, and given Rajput genealogy as the Agnicular or "fire-born" race. The term Jāt is now universally accepted as referring to the Hindu Jat of Hindustan, and of Rajputana, Delhi, Rohtak, etc. Their history in the past has been that of a powerful warlike race, and in 1806 and 1826 they tried conclusions with the British, who twice besieged the Jāt fortress of Bhurtpore. The failure of Lord Lake after repeated and costly assaults, and the success of Lord Combermere, with a heavy battering-train, twenty years later, has been already referred to. It is not necessary to further describe them, except to say that they

10th Jāts.
A Jāt from Shekhawati.

are a fine sturdy race of cultivators, who till the
land while the Rajput looks on. They have been
long considered excellent horse soldiers, and of
late years class Jāt regiments have been carefully
recruited, while many regiments take Jāt companies
and squadrons. The 14th Cavalry (Murray's Jāt
Lancers) and the 6th and 10th Infantry are Jāt class
regiments, that is to say, Hindu Jats of Rajputana
and Hindustan. A reference to the Indian Army
List will show many other regiments with one or
more Jāt squadrons or companies. As with other
races, class enlistment has much improved their
military value. The Gūjars are also a people found
scattered in tribal communities far and wide over
India, and largely in the Punjab, in Kashmir, and
in Gujarat. They are also believed to be a
Scythian race known to history as the Yūchi, who
came into India slightly earlier than the Jāts.
They colonized both banks of the Indus from
Scinde to the Hazara district and spread to Gujarat,
Rajputana, and Delhi. In the Punjab they eventually adopted Islam, but had originally given up
their serpent worship for Hinduism. They have
of recent years been enlisted in certain class company regiments with success. They are largely
graziers in modern times, and to a great extent the

term Gūjar is applied to grazing people irrespective of their real race, just as Jăt is often applied to cultivator. They are a powerful, strong-featured race, best known to the European world from seeing those of them who feed their flocks on the Kashmir hills.

The Gurkha

The Gurkha differs very considerably in many ways from the ordinary soldier of the Indian Army. He is like the Hazaras, whom he closely resembles but for a difference in height, also the inhabitant of an independent kingdom. The term Gurkha is now applied to the majority of the inhabitants of the kingdom of Nepal, but in strict ethnography belongs to those races which formed part of the old kingdom of Gurkha, a comparatively small part of Nepal. The inhabitants of Nepal consist of varying races. There are the Aryan and Rajput clans who spread to Nepal to fight for kingdom and barony in the days when the Aryan Rajput and Brahman races spread over Hindustan, and also the Mongolian races whom they supplanted or conquered. In the early days of the enlistment of Gurkhas, only the Mongolian tribes were taken, and those chiefly from Central Nepal. Their

Hinduism was of the simplest, and, in fact, they were, and are, more Buddhist than Hindu. The principal tribes thus preferred were Magar and Gurung, of which there are many clans. As the demand for more men of Nepal increased, recruits were taken from the tribes of Eastern Nepal, known as Limbos and Rais, also belonging to tribes of Mongolian origin. Then the Nepalese of Aryan stock claiming Rajput origin have now been enlisted under the general name of "*Khas*" Gurkhas. They include what are known as the Khas tribes and the Thakurs. The principle of class and clan is here also strictly preserved and insisted on by the army authorities. The *Khas* Gurkhas go to one double - battalion regiment, the 9th, and Magars and Gurungs chiefly to the older regiments; Limbos and Rais to the newer corps. There are twenty battalions of Gurkhas in the service, as well as a few in the Guides and in the Kashmir Army. Their language is *Khas-khura*, which is somewhat similar to Hindi and is derived from the Sanskrit. Their enlistment dates from the days of the Nepal War, after which certain regiments took companies of them, and three local battalions were raised, viz. the Nasiri, the Sirmoor, and the Kumaon battalions. The Gurkha soldier is clothed as a rifleman and wears in moderate weather the old Kilmarnock cap, the universal army forage-cap of the Crimean days. The Magar and Gurung are short and powerful with a bullet-shaped Mongolian head. Limbos and Rais are taller, and the *Khas* approaches more to the Aryan height. The services of the Gurkha soldier generally, the intense camaraderie existing between himself and his officer, and between him and British troops who can forget their Saxon awkwardness, are well known. All are dressed in rifle green, while the 2nd, the old Sirmoor battalion, wears the same uniform as the 60th rifles, in memory of the day when they and the 60th held the exposed flank of the Ridge before Delhi, come rain and shine, against all comers from the first to the last of the famous siege. The 1st, 2nd, 3rd, 4th, 6th, and 9th Gurkhas are represented in the plates.

THE GARHWALI

The term Garhwali is a geographical one, being applied to the inhabitants of the country known as Garhwal, which hangs under the buttress of the Himalaya in the hills west of Nepal. The term in its military sense applies chiefly to the Khasia race, who are probably an aboriginal race absorbed to some extent by custom and intermingling with the Aryan Rajputs, and also certain purer Rajput immigrants. The Khasias demand, and are practically accorded, the status of Rajputs. Garhwalis, of the tribes and races referred to, were till comparatively recent years enlisted among the rank and file of ordinary Gurkha regiments, in which they gained considerable reputation as soldiers. The advance of ethnological knowledge resulted in their being separated very properly from Gurkhas, and gradually eliminated from Gurkha battalions. The 39th Bengal Infantry was finally made a class battalion of Garhwalis, and later a second battalion was added. The Garhwali battalions are dressed in the well-known Gurkha style of rifle uniform with Kilmarnock cap. Though not such soldiers by instinct as the Gurkha, they are a courageous hill-race who make active and obedient soldiers of considerable fighting value. They are a small people, but not so thick-set and muscular as the Gurkha.

Mahrattas

The Deccan, or country south of the river Narbudda, was among the last of the districts to which the early Aryan conquerors penetrated.

The Vindhya Mountains and the forests of the Deccan long harboured fabulous aboriginal tribes who were overcome only after years of difficult advance and struggle. This country was known as Maharashtra or Mahratta, and its principal population was either the Aryans who had absorbed many of the conquered tribes, or the original tribes only tempered with a leaven of Brahmanism. The Mahrattas of to-day and of modern Indian history claim somewhat vaguely to be Rajputs, and no doubt one of those mysterious absorptions of a newly conquered race did take place, as in the case of Scythian-descended agnicular Rajputs. The Mahrattas, the inhabitants of modern Maharashtra, are the land-owning class of the Deccan proper, viz. the high plateau and the seaboard of western India. They first came into fame in the struggle made by Sivaji, a Mahratta of the Bhonsla family, to overthrow the power of the Muhammadans and restore a Hindu *Raj*. This rôle as the champions of Hinduism, to this day attaches to them to some extent. The history of the successes of Sivaji, the " mountain rat," in his struggles against the power of Islam, the growth of the Mahratta power and confederacy, their seizure of the person of the great Mogul, their defeat and slaughter by the

Afghans, near the " Black Mango tree " at Paniput, are all famous in the history of India.   Well known also is the long series of wars which they insisted on waging against the British and their allies, to their undoing.   Several of the famous Mahratta chiefs of the old confederacy, however, still rule over feudatory States.   The Mahrattas are divided, in modern parlance, into Dekhani and Konkhani, the former from the upland plateau east of the great mountains of the Ghats, the latter the inhabitants of the seaboard.   They have long served with credit and distinction in the Bombay Army, and several class regiments exist, while several others have class companies and squadrons.   The Mahrattas have a reputation for great wiriness and endurance. The 103rd, 105th, 110th, 114th, 116th, and 117th Infantry are Mahratta regiments, each enlisting six companies of Mahrattas and only two companies of other classes.   Marathi is an offshoot from the Sanskrit, and is spoken by many people of the Deccan who are not Mahrattas.   Mahratta Brahmans are merely Brahmans who have dwelt for many centuries in Maharasthra, and have developed an extreme reputation for ability and intrigue.   In the days of the Mahratta Confederacy they wielded much of the power in the various offices of state, a lost position to which no doubt they are keenly alive.

THE MUHAMMADANS OF INDIA

Reference has already been made in previous chapters, and in the foregoing notes on various races, to the different classes of Muhammadans within India, both those who have been converted to Islam from among the races of India, such as the Muhammadan Rajputs, and those who have entered India and settled there in the train of the various Muhammadan conquerors. The Musalman races of the Punjab have been described at length. Throughout India are to be found those who claim foreign descent and who are putatively either Pathan, Mogul, Sheikh, or Saiyid. Pathan and Mogul are recognizable as descendants of conquering races; Saiyids or elders are properly the descendants of Fatima, daughter of the Prophet; while Sheikhs are members of the Koreish tribe to which the Prophet belonged. Converts of low caste, however, have constantly claimed to belong to one of these races. Muhammadans who claim to be of these races are therefore enlisted more if they come of land-owning and cultivating stock than for any purely race claim, while, of course, the

Muhammadan Rajput tribes, such as the Rangars from the neighbourhood of Delhi, are freely enlisted. They are all taken into class companies and squadrons, more in accordance with the province they reside in than with racial distinction, viz. as "Muhammadans of Rajputana," etc.   The descendants of Pathán and Mogul settlers, who are clearly recognizable as such, make splendid cavalry soldiers, and in the past have been most distinguished in the irregular cavalry.   The 5th Light Infantry and the 17th and 18th Infantry are class regiments of Musalmans of the Eastern Punjab and Hindustan, and the 1st Skinner's Horse is entirely composed of Muhammadans of the Eastern Punjab, Delhi, and Hindustan, many of Rajput descent, while all the Indian cavalry regiments from 1 to 8 have one or more squadrons of this class.

The Military Races of the Carnatic

Constant references have been made in the preceding chapters to the services of the Coast Army—the Army of the Madras Presidency—and the various recruiting experiments that have been resorted to, to obtain satisfactory recruits fit for modern conditions of war.   Most of the experiments with special races, such as men of the Coorg hills and that strange Arab-descended race the Moplahs, have been abandoned. The recasting of the three armies into one Line enabled the authorities to proceed with the question purely on its merits as part of one general policy. It was possible to resist the feelings and sentiment of the older officers of the Madras Army, who had that natural attachment of the British officer for the classes and men they have so long led, and definitely decide on the number of regiments to be recruited from the Madras Presidency. The Madras Army had for some years been divided into two portions in the minds of the authorities, viz. in one the sapper and miner and pioneer corps, and the other the ordinary Tamil and Madrasi Musalman corps.

The two former classes of corps had long enlisted men of the artizan classes ready to go anywhere, eat anything, and turn their hands to anything. They had been famous for useful semi-military service in many parts, and were eminently desirable. The actual number of Line battalions was to be restricted to eight, and these, with the three pioneer corps and the corps of sappers and miners, with about half a squadron in each of the three Light Cavalry regiments, were alone to enlist men of

Madras. The reduction of the demand on recruiting centres has naturally enabled corps to raise their physical and mental standard for recruits.

The military races of Madras consist of the Tamils and the Muhammadans. The Tamils and other Hindus are of the Dravidian races who were only affected by the Aryan invasion many centuries after the rest of India.   Brahman and Rajput blood and influence have to some extent affected them as it did all the original races that the Aryans met, but only to a small extent. The Tamils are divided into many classes and castes. One large caste, the Telinga or Telegus, are now no longer enlisted, though at one time serving in considerable numbers. An outcaste race, the Parraiyans or Pariahs, have long been enlisted, especially in the pioneers and sappers, and to a small extent in all corps, and have many useful qualities.

The Muhammadans consist, as in other parts of India, of the converted races and those who claim foreign descent, Pathan, Mogul, Sheikh, or Saiyid. To these, as elsewhere, converts have always tried to claim affinity. The Muhammadans who enlist in the cavalry are probably nearer to the Pathan than anything else, coming as a rule from Vellore, round which most of the descendants of Hyder

Ali's following are to be found. Hyder Ali himself was of the foreign-adventurer breed.

The soldiers of Madras have many inherent military qualities. They shoot well, drill well, and stand well under arms, and so far as this part of their professional requirement goes, foreign critics have been known to say that it was not till they got to Madras that they saw regular native soldiers. The eight Carnatic battalions of the Line enlist 4 companies Muhammadans, 2 companies Tamils, 2 companies Pariahs.

CHAPTER VI

In Chapter IV. the reconstruction after the great Mutiny was traced, with the gradual evolution of the carefully calculated modern system of enlistment, and in Chapter V. the various military castes and clans as recognized to-day. When Lord Kitchener came to India, the whole army stood in four subordinate armies, yclept commands, under the one Commander-in-Chief. The regiments of the three presidential armies still retained their old numbers, with the resulting multiplication of similarly numbered units already described. The Empire had just been through a war on a large scale. Russia and Japan were at war, and war and the dangers of unpractical or complicated organization, or the lack of it, were uppermost in everyone's minds. Armies must either be organized for the immediate business of war or must be abolished.

So in the many changes that this spirit was working in the Empire, there was enough driving force to overcome the valuable though at times dangerous attachment to old names and old principles.

The fiat went forth that the old armies were to be renumbered on one roster, and that the Bengal Army, though not the oldest, should stand first on the roster, followed by the Punjab Frontier Force, then the old Coast Army of Madras, then the Hyderabad Contingent, and lastly, the famous faithful old Army of Bombay. To minimize the blow, and to bear testimony to the fact that the authorities were not hopelessly blind to the value of military sentiment, the opportunity was taken to give to corps titles connecting them with the officers who had raised them, or with their early history, or some suitable title of a similar nature.

The regiments of the Bengal Army therefore headed the Line, both Cavalry and Infantry. To enable corps to keep their own digits, that is to say, corps that were originally one to still have the figure one among their number, each army began its numbering as the first of a series. Thus the numbering of the Bengal Army and the Frontier Force stopped at 59. The number 60 was left vacant, and the old 1st Madras Infantry became the 61st, and the old 1st Bombay Grenadiers became the 101st Grenadiers. Those numbers that had been vacant owing to the disbanding of corps after the Afghan wars were left vacant so as not to disturb the digit of those corps following it. Occasion, however, was taken to bring into the vacant numbers one or two corps that had been recently raised. The Frontier Force was partly accounted for in a similar way, the numbers 49 and 50 being left vacant, and the 1st Sikhs became the 51st Sikhs (Frontier Force). The Punjab Infantry of the Frontier Force and the Hyderabad regiments had to lose even this much trace of their older numbers, but the Frontier Force Cavalry were enabled to take up the numbers from 21 onwards.

Shortly after this the 9th Bengal Infantry (Khas Gurkhas) were removed from the general Line, and put into the separate Gurkha Line, as the 9th Gurkhas, while the 42nd, 43rd, and 44th Light Infantry Gurkhas who had been localized in Assam were also brought into the Gurkha numbering, and their place in the Line taken by certain special irregular battalions that had existed as local corps in Central India. The old 10th Madras

Infantry, changed in 1890 to a Gurkha battalion, finally became the 10th Gurkhas.

The result of this renumbering was as follows :—

The Cavalry

First the Cavalry of the Line received their present numbering from 1 to 39, without break, except that the number of the old 4th Punjab Cavalry of the Frontier Force, reduced after the Afghan War, has been left vacant and there is no 24. The two regiments of the Central India Horse, famous relic of the numerous irregular horse that the suppression of the Mutiny called forth in Central India, or composed of loyal remnants, received the numbers 38 and 39. These with the Guides Cavalry, an independent squadron in the Deoli and Erinpura Irregular corps, the Aden troop, and the three Bodyguard corps form the regular cavalry of India. The 26th, 27th, and 28th are Light Cavalry, and are non-Silladar. They are, that is to say, troopers, mounted on Government horses as are the British Cavalry. They are the only survivals of the Light Cavalry of the pre - Mutiny days, and still wear the French grey and silver of the older times. Only three of the cavalry regiments are " class " corps, viz. the 1st Skinner's Horse, composed entirely of Muhammadans of Hindustan and the Southern Punjab; the 14th Murray's Jāt Lancers, entirely of Jāts; and the 15th Cureton's Multanis, entirely of Multani Pathans and kindred neighbouring races. The remainder of the regiments consist of class squadrons, of which the principal divisions are Sikhs, Dogras, Pathans, Punjabi, Hindustani, or Dekhani Muhammadans, Jats, and Rajputs. The various plates of the men of these regiments depict one or other of these classes, and clearly show the distinctive features and methods of wearing the lungi (head-dress) of each race. The cavalry soldier generally comes from the more wealthy cultivating and land-owning members of the classes described.

17th Infantry (The Loyal Regiment).
A Rajput from Hissar.

Of the exploits of the various regiments it is impossible to speak here; suffice it to say that they are numerous and varied, but that the fact that many of the corps date from the Mutiny accounts for the shorter tally of fame of some. The Indian Army List details the class composition, the previous history, the uniform, and the battle honours of each corps. A few may perhaps be referred to as typical. The 1st of the post-Mutiny Line, formerly the old 1st Irregulars, was raised by the famous half-breed James Skinner, long affectionately known to his friends in the army as "Old Sekunder." It practically came over to the British in 1803 from the remnant of the De Boigne-trained Mahratta Army. After much service in the pacification of India in the early days, it marched to Kandahar in the First Afghan War, having previously taken part in the storming and capture of Bhurtpore. Its later services have been in the last Afghan War, and the relief of Pekin in 1900. The 2nd Gardner's Horse has a history nearly as old, having been raised in 1809, and later numbered as the 2nd Irregulars; while the 3rd are also Skinner's Horse, having been the second of two Risalahs raised by Colonel James Skinner. The 3rd took part also in the First Afghan War, while the 2nd served in the First Burmese War and both the Sikh wars. The 1st is noted for its uniform of bright canary, the fancy of "Old Sekunder." In the Skinner Church at Delhi is a stone on which is

सुं मे सन्तवीर गुरुं २/२ गोरखा

टेक्का ठाकर खत्री
A. C. LOVETT

A.C.LOVETT.

A.C.LOVETT

recorded the name of all the commandants of the corps. The Mutiny record of most of the corps is more than distinguished. Of late years, the 11th in Swat in 1897, and the 13th led by Atkinson, in a timely charge over extremely bad ground at a critical moment at Shabkadr, have given evidence of the dash that is inherent in this branch of the Service. The Guides perhaps have found opportunity to enhance their own and the Sirkar's fame, more than has been vouchsafed to other corps. No opportunity was ever wasted, from the days of the staunch old native officer who knew no more drill than the principle of the attack contained in " Draaw swaards and Hulla," to the accomplished and equally dashing modern trooper. Their charge at Fattehabad, when another Battye fulfilled his weird, the hopeless, dogged defence of the Residency at Kabul, in the last Afghan War, the repeated charges in Swat in '97, were all opportunities for service rendered and honour gained that were seized to the full. The cavalry of the Frontier Force, since their formation, have spent a life of raid and counter-raid on the border : an eye for an eye and a tooth for a tooth, which is always border law. Among many incidents might be recalled the charge of the 25th Cavalry, Vousden leading, at the King's Garden near Sherpore, in the Afghan War. When we come to the three Light Cavalry regiments, the 26th, 27th, and 28th, we touch the very origin of Indian military history so far as the British are concerned, from Sholinghur and the Carnatic wars to Seringapatam and Mahidpore, and then on through the last century. Two out of the cavalry regiments of the old Hyderabad Contingent served in the burning Central India Campaign. The 31st to the 37th, the cavalry of the Bombay Army, have a long record, of which perhaps the 33rd charging the Persian squares at Kooshab in 1857, and the 34th, when newly raised, sharing in the famous stand against the Peshwa's hordes at Corygaum, are the most notable.

The Indian Artillery

The Indian artillery of to-day consists of twelve mountain batteries numbered from 21 to 32. The lower numbers are borne by the British mountain batteries, of which there are eight, with vacant numbers to spare for any possible increase. The first four Indian batteries are the old light field batteries and mountain trains of the Frontier Force ; 25 and 26 are of older origin, being the only relic of the native artillery of the Company's army, formerly numbers 1 and 2 companies of Bombay Golandaz.   The remainder are of more recent origin, 27 and 28 having been raised at the time of the Third Burmese War, with the original numbering of 1 and 2 Bengal mountain batteries.   All the Indian mountain batteries consist of Punjabis, half Muhammadan and half Hindu, the latter being almost entirely Sikhs.   The gunners are specially selected for their height and strength, with a view to the rapid assembling and dismantling of the guns from off and on to the backs of the powerful mules that carry them.   Mountain artillery is practically a special arm peculiar to India so far as our army is concerned, and has long been famous for its mountaineering capacity. The services of this branch of the artillery are more than notable.   The 21st, 22nd, and 24th batteries in the last Afghan War, the 22nd in the Kurram and on the Samana, the 25th at Maizar in Waziristan, and the 28th at the Malakand and in Bajour in the '97-'98 frontier campaigns, gained more than average distinction.   On the frontier one more artillery corps exists, formerly known as the Punjab Garrison Battery, and familiarly the " Blokes " (owing to its being formed of veterans from the mountain batteries past their prime on the hillside), now the Frontier Garrison Artillery. Their name describes their rôle. A plate shows the mountaineer gunner.

In addition to these mountain batteries, reference must be made to the Indian soldiers serving as a portion of the European batteries of artillery. The horse and field batteries have a few native drivers, while the ammunition columns, which are fully horsed in India, have native drivers and native gunners as waggon - men. The British mountain batteries have British gunners and all native drivers. The heavy batteries similarly have British gunners and native drivers. These men are enlisted from the usual fighting classes of the Punjab. A few come from Hindustan. The drivers of the mountain batteries have long been established, and have acquired a high reputation. Those in the heavy batteries and ammunition columns are a comparatively new experiment. Driving powerful " Waler " horses is quite different work from leading mules, which is what mountain artillery driving consists of, but the men promise to be as good at the one as the other. It is in the artillery alone that British and Indian personnel serve together, and the two races do succeed in striking a happy *modus vivendi*. In the mountain batteries many of the drivers are old soldiers with several campaigns to their credit.   Atkins is wont to borrow their bemedalled tunics to be photographed in, which is a fair token of camaraderie.

THE ENGINEERS

The rank and file of the Royal Engineers do not come to India save for a few non-commissioned officers attached to sapper companies.   The engineer services are, therefore, all Indian, so far as the men are concerned, and consist of several consecutively numbered companies grouped into three corps, which corps are the lawful successors without break of the three famous engineer corps of the three Presidencies.

62nd Punjabis, Subadar.
A Dhund from Rawal Pindi.

The 1st Prince of Wales' Own Sappers and Miners are the old Bengal Sappers and Miners, and consist of six service companies and various attached special sections.   They enlist Sikhs, Pathans, Punjabi Muhammadans, and a few Hindustanis of various classes. Their battle honours include every campaign of any importance since the storming of Bhurtpore. The 2nd Queen's Own Sappers and Miners are the old Madras Sappers and Miners, with headquarters at Bangalore, and consist also of six service companies, with one company localized in Burma and enlisting Burmese. The remainder enlist Madrasis. Several special sections are also attached to this corps. Their war record is even more complete than that of the 1st, and commences from a far earlier date. The 3rd Sappers and Miners are the old Bombay Sappers and Miners, consisting of six service companies and a fortress company with certain special sections. The class composition of the companies is very varied, and Sikhs, Mahrattas, Rajputs, and Muhammadans are all drawn on. Their record also is varied and distinguished, commencing from the fight at Beni-Boo-Ali in 1823 on the shores of the Persian Gulf.

The British officers of the Sapper Corps are, of course, Royal Engineers, with a few N.C.O.'s from the corps for special duties.

Four divisional signal companies have been added recently to the army with the object of managing all the signal services of a division (one company per division) in the field. These companies have also been formed as engineer units, and their personnel, though drawn from the army at large, are classed and rated for the time being as Sappers.

THE INFANTRY

The infantry, as has been explained, is numbered in two separate lines — the ordinary Line and the Gurkha Line. The Line itself consists of battalions numbered from 1 to 130, of which 14 numbers are vacant, and one, the 39th Garhwal Rifles, is a double-battalion corps. That is to say, that 117 battalions remain, and the infantry of the Guides. In the Gurkha Line there are ten two-battalion regiments, numbered 1 to 10; thus the total number of battalions of Indian Infantry is 138.

The constitution of them under the careful system of class recruiting has now resulted as follows :—

41 class-company Punjabi battalions, in which the classes are some variation of Muhammadan, Sikh, Pathan, or Dogra.

9 Sikh battalions, of which three enlist Mazbi Sikhs.

3 Dogra battalions.
2 Brahman class battalions.
7 battalions of Hindu Rajputs from outside the Punjab.
2 Jat (Hindu) battalions.
28 class-company battalions, of which the classes are not exclusively from the Punjab.
6 purely Muhammadan battalions, of which three are from outside the Punjab, and three exclusively from the Punjab and the transfrontier.
6 Mahratta battalions, exclusively Mahrattas save for two companies of Dekhani Muhammadans each.
1 battalion of Afghan Hazaras.
1 two-battalion regiment of Garhwalis.
11 battalions recruited from the classes of the Carnatic.
20 battalions of Gurkhas.

Of these battalions, 12 are pioneers with special training in road and rail making and rough engineering work, and equipped to that end, but also trained as infantry. India alone of the British Empire has pioneer corps, since India alone expects campaigns by way of goat-tracks and mountain watercourses.

The foregoing describes the fighting troops of the Indian Army, which, with the British troops forming part of the garrison, are combined into formations of the Imperial war organization, being grouped by brigades into divisions. The war organization of the Empire is by strong three-brigade divisions with brigades of mounted troops, and the Empire has practically copied India in discarding thoughts of army corps, and preferring to find the force required by the grouping of strong divisions. This Indian Army of British and Indian regiments and batteries is able to furnish nine war divisions and several cavalry brigades, after furnishing the internal garrisons for the support of peace and order and the civil power. But since an army crawls on its belly, and masses of battalions and regiments and batteries do not make an army, or even divisions of it, administrative troops are an essential component. A quarter column of bakers' carts does not convey the pomp of war, though a file of ambulances may suggest the pity of it, yet these are the services that make men with muskets into an army, and should not be forgotten in the tally for their more outwardly effective comrades.

The administrative troops of India are principally the Indian Subordinate Medical Service, the Army Hospital Corps, the Army Bearer Corps, and the Supply and Transport Corps.   None of these are in themselves war formations. That is to say, they do not exist, with certain exceptions as regards Transport Corps, as units that take the field in the same formation as they stand in peace time, as do the fighting troops of an army. They exist as corps which form, as it were, a pool from which war units are mobilized. The Army Bearer Corps, for instance, supplies the bearers for regimental ambulance carriage and also for the field ambulances. The Supply and Transport Corps mobilizes the various supply units that accompany a force in the field. The men of the bearer corps are enlisted from that class, or, rather, those classes who are hereditary bearers by caste and practice. India for ever has been a land without roads, as we know the term, and even when trunk roads and railways traverse it, the majority of the villages are off the road along tracks. Brides and bridegrooms, who form the pageant of the East, and purdah ladies, and corpulent folk in general, have ever been carried. Therefore has a caste of hereditary carriers existed from time immemorial. Special thews and sinews to lift the weight and bear its pressure have developed, and from these classes alone do good bearers come. The change of life that is so rapidly coming over the East, as a result of the energy and movement of the West, is decreasing the men who are, by profession, bearers, especially in Oudh, whence come the Hindu Kahars, who are the best. There is a question connected with bearers which illustrates one of the difficulties of organization in India.   The rules of caste being specially strict where food and drink are concerned, the wounded Hindu will starve or die rather than take food or water from an unfit man.   The Kahar of Oudh, however, is an hereditary servant, and from him almost all Hindu soldiers will take food and water. Efficient bearer corps should, therefore, contain this class, for, if chance bearers are entertained in war-time, apart from their physical incapacity to carry the dandies, fighting men have to be taken from the ranks to tend Hindu soldiers in hospital.   The devotion of good bearers to the wounded they carry has often been borne testimony to.

The Transport Corps are of several kinds, and these do exist to some extent as permanent war formations, but many corps, of course, are mobilized from reserve and registered animals.   The majority of the transport personnel comes from the Punjab, either from smaller-sized men of the classes enlisted in the regiments, or from the lesser clans and castes.   Mules and camels being more bred and used in the Punjab than elsewhere, it is but natural to enlist from the classes used to them. There are two varieties of camel corps which are interesting.   They are the Silladar Corps and the

Grantee Corps. Silladar Camel Corps are raised somewhat on the same principle as the silladar cavalry. Camel-owners are paid a sum down to serve with their own camels. The troops of the camel corps have two rates of pay, an employed and an unemployed rate. They are called up by troops for work at times during the year, and at other times are doing their own work at their homes on unemployed pay. Grantee Camel Corps are furnished by men who have received grants of land on the new canal lands in the Punjab on condition of producing certain camels whenever required. They are embodied for a short period each year. The Camel Corps men come from the Muhammadan tribes—Baluch, Jat, etc.—of the sand and karoo-like plains between the Ravi, the Jhelum, the Chenab, and the Indus. The march of irrigation is, however, driving the camel from off the land. The camel-owners are wild, picturesque, long-haired rogues, almost as weird as their camels.

CHAPTER VII

IT is often forgotten that the portion of British
India that is not under direct rule is almost as
large as the portion that is.   The Indian feudatory
chiefs are many, and the extent of their territories
is in some cases very considerable.   The nature of
their tenure varies in almost every case, in accordance with treaties and sanads granted or entered
on during the course of the rise of our power; it
has ever been our policy to adhere rigidly to our
treaty obligations.   Circumstances at times have
caused us to go back on them, but in every case
those circumstances seemed at the time to have
been forced on us.   Native States that occupied
themselves with their own affairs, and did not
engage in the numerous intrigues and coalitions to
expel the foreigner, are still our trusted allies, as
favoured now and unmolested as when we first

entered into relations with them, little dreaming of the extent to which our rule would extend. The Nizam of Hyderabad is a case in point. It is more than a century ago since the Nizam was guaranteed protection from the Mahrattas and other encroaching neighbours, and compelled to get rid of his French allies as the price of protection. Since those days the relations between his State and the sovereign power have remained practically unchanged.

At the end of the 18th century the independent States, as well as the Feudatory States, had large armies organized to some extent on European lines. French, English, Italian, and American officers— some adventurers, others deputed officers—were training and commanding these State armies. They often led the armies of their respective masters into action against each other. Scindia's and the Nizam's services were organized on lines resembling our own. De Boigne, the Savoyard, in the service of Scindia, Maharaja of Gwalior State, had a regular establishment and cadet service like the Company's; the Nizam's service was similarly organized. Later Ranjit Singh, the Maharaja of the Punjab, had a similar service, while Golab Singh of Jammu and Kashmir organized many corps on the same lines.

The armies of these States were entirely separate from the various contingents which were officered by officers of the Company's Army, and were only a portion of the State forces in so far as the State concerned paid for them, or assigned districts to the British to pay for them.   To this day the State armies preserve some trace of the days when their armies were organized on European lines to enable them to oppose, if necessary, the irresistible force of the trained British sepoy.   They even preserve the dress of the early Victorian period.

The large armies that some of the States maintained, were at one time a source of anxiety to the supreme government, as much for the unnecessary drain on the resources of the States as for their possible danger in the event of disturbance, for their discipline was never as a rule in a satisfactory state.   They, however, represented the outward and visible sign of power and dominion to the rulers, and as such were naturally dear to them.   In the Mutiny some of the troops of the native States were able to render excellent service, especially those of the Cis Sutlej States, Jind and Patiala and Nabha, in keeping the road open from the Punjab to Delhi.   In Rajputana, too, their services were freely given.

Now and again since the Mutiny, if not before, discussion had taken place as to what was a fair contribution, if any, of native States towards the expense of the protection under which they flourished. It is not a century and a half since the

Sadul Light Infantry.   Havildar.
A Rahtor Rajput of Bikaner.

great invasions from the north had ceased to flow across the Indus to loot and to slay. To the smaller States the Mahratta pretensions and power were always a menace and a nightmare, and to the larger the terror of the north was never absent. It had been argued that they owed some assistance to the government that gave them peace, and, in the case of many, a protection from outside that they had never known before. In the slow progress of evolution that was going on, it was well to let things develop by themselves. The dangers of a large war, however, so strongly brought home to all in India after the Penjdeh incident, impressed on the rulers of the States how necessary it was that they should stand in with the supreme government in some of the burden of military preparation. 1885 saw half the army in India on the move to the Bolan, and immense sums were spent in preparing for a war that seemed inevitable. The Nizam of Hyderabad offered a large sum from his revenues to Government in aid of the war chest. His patriotic and spontaneous example was promptly followed by others. Government, however, did not feel that a contribution to the war chest was so desirable as an entry into some share of empire by the maintenance of a portion of the troops required for defence. From, therefore, the Penjdeh incident and the patriotic offers of the Feudatory States, sprang what is now known as the Imperial Service Troops. Government suggested that, in lieu of money offers, some portion of the troops in each State should be trained and improved so as to be fit to take their place in the field alongside the Indian Line. The offer was very eagerly accepted, and there had already from time to time been proposals put forward for organizing some of the State troops.

The result of this movement has been that almost every State of any size has contributed a force. These troops are in the same relation to their rulers as the older and less-organized corps from which they were formed. The Government offered up-to-date arms, and lent officers to train the troops. From the first beginnings has risen a force of many thousand men. The service of training and inspecting has been for many years thoroughly organized. An officer was appointed Inspector-General of Imperial Service Troops, with a staff of inspecting officers and assistant inspecting officers, who are in no way the servants of the States. They are deputed to assist in the training of the troops, to advise the Durbars (the official terms for the State governments) on military matters connected with the troops, and to see that they generally do attain that standard of efficiency that will justify the authorities in accepting them as part of the recognized contingent. The States are grouped into circles for this purpose, and an inspecting officer with assistants presides over each, and visits each State in turn.

The result of this experiment has been a happy one. In addition to providing a satisfactory career for the feudal gentry of the States, it has brought the best class of sirdar into touch with the best class of British officer. The States are lavish in their offer of troops for service whenever there is a war or threat of war. The Imperial Service Troops have been engaged in many operations since 1895. The Relief of Chitral, Tirah, the campaign across the Swat river, the Mohmand Expedition, Somaliland, China, have all been shared with State troops. In the South African War, since their troops could not share, horses and equipment in charge of State personnel were freely sent.

The State of Kashmir enjoys a peculiar position in that it not only marches with the outer boundary, but with, or practically with, a part of the Russian frontier, which is an entirely different condition from that obtaining in other States. Her troops therefore garrison her own frontier districts, and have constantly been engaged with tribes on her border, and have seen a very considerable amount of frontier service. The defence of Chitral was largely carried out by the Kashmir troops; while in the Hunza Nagar campaign they bore a considerable share in the earliest days of their organization on modern lines. Kashmir alone has Imperial Service Artillery, two mountain batteries being organized principally for the defence of the Gilgit frontier. One, however, took part in the Tirah Expedition of 1897-98.

The upkeep of highly trained and well-equipped troops costs more than the older units they replaced, which for fifty years had purely existed for guard and ceremonial purposes. The various States, therefore, while retaining what are styled their regular troops, have in most cases considerably reduced their numbers to meet the extra cost of the Imperial Service Corps.

It will be remembered how, in the days of the Mutiny, several rulers, who staunchly maintained the British authority in every way in their power, were themselves betrayed by the action either of their contingents or of their other troops. The contingents, it should be remembered, were bodies of troops maintained by treaty for their own protection, officered by British officers. In most parts of India these contingents were not recruited from the population of the State whose troops they titularly were. They were not actuated by personal loyalty to their chief, but were largely drawn from what had become so universal a recruiting - ground, viz. Oudh and Behar. They followed the example of the Bengal Army, and not of their ruler. The leading case is that of the famous Gwalior Contingent as well as the other troops of Scindia. The Gwalior Contingent was one of the *élite* forces in India. The loyalty of Scindia was beyond dispute and his actions were unequivocal, but his mercenary troops and the contingent followed the prevailing wind. It has therefore been decreed that the Imperial Service Troops shall be subjects of the ruler they serve, so that they may be expected to follow his lead and that of no one else. Certain exceptions are allowed to this rule, notably in Kashmir, where it has been the custom, far older than our days, for Gurkhas to serve in considerable numbers in that State. An Imperial Service and also a regular battalion in Kashmir enlist a large number of the men of Nepal.

In many States the rulers themselves command their own corps, or appoint their sons and relatives to do so, so that these troops are Royal Troops in the old - fashioned sense of the word, and the feudal spirit and system does really exist. A plate shows the Maharaja of Bikaner, a Rajput of famous race, as the Colonel-in-Chief of one of his own Imperial Service Corps. It is no uncommon thing to see the chiefs lead their troops in review past some high authority, with a dash that they are equally prepared to maintain in the field.

The corps of a State army bear names reminiscent of the names in the days of the Mogul forces. The regiment of the sun, the battalion of victory, the lightning battery are common terms. The regular forces, as distinct from the Imperial Service, have the arms and equipment and often the clothing of the early Victorian or Georgian period, and at a review in some State capital one is able to step back a couple of generations. Side by side with the troops of an old régime, are the highly trained, modern-armed troops of the Imperial Service, which stand on parade as stand the troops of the Indian Army. The uniforms, especially the full dress, are more elaborate in many cases than our own, and the Imperial Service cavalry are often superbly dressed, especially the officers. For manœuvre and service the dress is of course the regulation khaki and plain accoutrements of India. It has taken years to inculcate the principle in all armies, that however you may dress your troops in glory for gala occasions, the war dress must be as simple and easy as possible; and yet nothing betrays more clearly the strength of purpose behind a disciplined army than the mass of loosely clad active men in a drab or khaki dust-proof dress.

It will be convenient to refer to the troops of each State in the circles to which they are arranged for the convenience of inspection and expert advice, at the hands of the Government of India, as these circles are grouped for geographical reasons.

The status of these States, however, should be first explained. Their relations to the Army and to the Government are practically those of the troops of allies. The States offer to maintain troops on our model, we promise to assist, and then in times of stress and strain the States place them at His Majesty's disposal. The troops are subject to the military law of the States both in peace and war, which is assimilated to the Indian Articles of War (recently remodelled into the Indian Army Act). The disciplinary Acts of the States, however, enact in most cases that the commander of the British force in the field, with which they are acting, shall be the higher legal authority referred to for the various purposes of the Acts. The situation is therefore clear and understandable.

The State maintaining the largest contingent is Jammu and Kashmir, which has one squadron, two mountain batteries, and three battalions of infantry.

The frontier conditions peculiar to this State demand a considerable force, and in the days when Chitral and Hunza were more prominent factors, the number of battalions was six. Reference has been already made to the peculiarity of this State, for historical reasons, enlisting aliens, viz. Gurkhas. Next to Kashmir, or perhaps equal to it, is Gwalior. It has three regiments of lancers and two battalions of infantry, with a strong transport train of 300 carts.   The latter corps has often taken part in frontier expeditions. The Maharaja Scindia being himself an enthusiastic and well-read soldier, this force benefits by a considerable share of his personal attention. Outside these two States it will be simpler to refer to the States according to the circles already referred to. In the Punjab we have Patiala with one regiment of cavalry and two of infantry, of whom the first took part in the frontier campaign of

9th Bhopal Infantry. Subadar-Major.
A Suni Musalman.

1897 ; Nabha, Kapurthala, and Jind, the other Sikh States, each furnish a battalion of infantry ; while Bahawalpore furnishes a camel transport corps of 966 camels, properly disciplined, with its own mounted escort as a military camel corps. The action of the Sikh States, in keeping open the road to Delhi in 1857, by which the Punjab was able to send down its men and material unmolested, is a matter of history.   In the Multan rising in 1848, it was the Daudputras, the troops of Bahawalpore, who first came up to assist Herbert Edwardes, alone with his levies and doubtful Durbar troops from the Derajat.   Sirmoor, Malerkotla, and Faridkot each maintain a company of sappers and miners, a form of contingent as specially useful as the transport corps.   Tehri, a State in the hills of Garhwal, also maintains a company of sappers.   Alwar maintains a regiment of lancers and a battalion of infantry.   Bharatpur (the Bhurtpore of earlier history) has a battalion and a transport corps.   Rajputana and the Rajput States are naturally the centre of loyal service and soldierly instinct.   Bikaner has a battalion and a camel corps 500 strong, which served both in China and Somaliland.   Jodhpore has two lancer corps, the famous Sardar Rissalah, with the bluest blood in

Rajputana in its ranks. Jaipore has a double-strength transport corps of 550 carts. Rampore maintains two squadrons of lancers ; Junagarh and Navanagaar and Udaipore each maintain a squadron of lancers. The Muhammadan State of Bhopal has a lancer regiment, Bhavanagar has two Rajput squadrons, and Indore a transport corps with an escort squadron. Down in the Deccan and farther south, the movement still holds good. The ancient State, and our ancient ally Hyderabad, has two regiments of cavalry, and Mysore a cavalry regiment and a transport corps.

The total then of this force voluntarily organized by the more important States as the best way of contributing their share to the burden of empire is as follows : Cavalry, ten regiments of four squadrons each, and one of three squadrons, with eight squadrons in corps of lesser strength than three squadrons. Infantry, six eight-company battalions and six six-company battalions ; then two mountain batteries, four companies of sappers, five mule or pony cart transport corps aggregating 1650 army carts, two camel transport corps aggregating 1200 camels, a fighting camel corps of 500 rifles, and three transport escorts for the protection of transport corps provided by the State. This force means a very considerable accession of fighting strength, while the transport corps and sappers are an asset far above their actual numbers in value.

Such in outline are the forces maintained by the feudatories of India, forces which are now enlisted on the same class lines as the Indian Army, and which are composed of the races already referred to in Chapter IV. The uniform has already been referred to as being of the same general style as the Indian Army, and of the same simplicity in its field service order, but more varied, and more elaborate in its full dress. More varied, because a dozen or so different States are concerned ; more elaborate, because they often form troops necessary to the ceremony of the various households. Among the plates will be found the uniforms of the Bikaner Camel Corps, the Jodhpore, Alwar, and Mysore Lancers, and some of the chiefs who lead them. It is in the feudatory courts, especially at the Rajput courts that felt the Mogul influence the least, that the old traditions and customs of the Hindu kingdoms of centuries ago are still to be seen ; while in Rajputana itself, the old Rajput chivalry, with pride of race and pride of weapons, still remains, and hence provides a mounted soldier second to none. How long in the process and change that railways are carrying to the uttermost ends of Hindustan, is a matter for reflection, and perhaps sad reflection. The lament of the days that are passing is to be read in Sir Alfred Lyall's verses, and there are many who mourn the days that are going—

When I rode a Dekhani charger with the saddle-cloth gold laced,
And a Persian sword and a twelve-foot spear, and a pistol at my
  waist.
My son he keeps a pony and I grin to see him astride,
Jogging away to the market and swaying from side to side.

And again, the old Rajput chief:

I cannot learn in an English school,
Yet the hard word softens and change is best.
My sons must leave the ancient ways,
The folk are weary, the land shall rest,
And the gods are kind for I end my days.

It is from the Feudatory States, and above all from Rajputana, that the born horse-soldier comes; for the legend of the hand keeping the head is barely dead a generation. Hard knocks and border law, the *Schwartzreiter* and the baron, are the factors that make the horse-soldier and the men-at-arms from the cradle. In British India, even the tradition is almost gone, so quickly does peace enter into a race's bones, but in the States the past is barely yet a legend. In British India, to make the yeoman and the peasant into the necessary number of citizen battalions and preserve as much as necessary of the old spirit, is the aim and object of the class by clan grouping that has been described.

CHAPTER VIII

CONCLUSION

" If the salt have lost its savour, wherewith shall it be seasoned ?"

THE foregoing completes the description of the regular native troops of India, though it does not comprise the whole tally of armed forces at the disposal of the Governor-General. A detailed description of these other forces is outside of the scope of the present work, but some allusion to them is necessary to complete an account of the Indian Army.

In all districts where the ordinary civil police with their truncheons and lockups do not suffice for the maintenance of law and order, some mailed fist is necessary. In ordinary places this is represented by the military garrison which is brought into play on rare occasions. In frontier districts where an uncivilized neighbour is always tempted by the wealth of others, and where the civil force is always an object of enmity, something between the wielder of the truncheon and the regular soldier is required. The requirements of armed escorts, armed arresting parties, treasure guards, and the like are harassing and undesirable for regular soldiers. In the thousand-mile-long marches of India from the Mekran coast round to the extremity of Burma, there exists, therefore, a semi-military force, entirely under the control of the civil power. This force exists in varying forms. It is most highly developed in the corps of the North-West Frontier militia, which under the command of army officers carries out the functions performed for many years by the Punjab Irregular Force. Its name is a misnomer, as it is a permanent force, on irregular lines, under the civil power. It is raised on the old border plan of "set a thief to catch a thief," on which the original Black Watch was raised. It is recruited, that is to say, from the border tribes. Two other varieties of irregulars exist on this portion of the frontier—they are the border military police, organized by battalions who hold the frontier posts, and the tribal levies. The levies are armed un-uniformed retainers of chiefs and headmen, who, in return for certain allowances, contract to police and protect certain roads and districts. The militia are more highly disciplined and trained than the border military police (known as the *barder*), and the *barder* are better than the *livy*. The levies are more familiarly known as "catchies," or "catch 'em alive ohs," not from their methods of catching raiders so much as for the mysteries of the tribal toilet.

Along the marches of Assam, which deals in large tribal frontiers, military police corps guard the frontier, while after the annexation of Upper Burma the necessary military garrison, if raised as regular troops of the Line, would have been costly in the extreme. A large force of military police, from the fighting races of India, was therefore raised on military lines, and largely assisted in the pacification of the country and the destruction of the bodies of armed dacoits into which the disbanded soldiers of Theebaw had resolved themselves. As the need for these corps diminished with the settling of the country, the best of them were taken into the Line, but a large number still remain for the necessary watching of the unadministered tribal tracts and the actual frontiers. The military police in Assam is largely recruited from Gurkhas or kindred races, and those now in Burma from the Punjab, but some of the local tribes also do excellent service. The total of this military police force, though scattered along many hundred miles of frontier, is very considerable.

After, therefore, due reference to this force that bears much of the burden of ordinary come-and-go on the borders, little remains but to review the Indian Army as it stands . . . one of the marvels of modern times. It is not profitable to consider at any time the question of its faithfulness, since the measure of the fidelity of this great force is the measure of the fidelity of all mercenary armies, that is to say, of all armies that serve voluntarily for a wage. We may rest content with the situation as it is, and the fact that so long as India as a whole acquiesces in our presence, and has faith in our prestige and our equity, and our power to give peace in the land, so long will the Indian Army continue to give us, and incidentally their own land, faithful military service. To expect more is to ask for the impossible. We may more profitably content ourselves with observing the marvellous nature of the glamour which the handful of English officers has from the earliest times been able to throw over these men of an alien race. The men of the Indian Army follow their alien officers with a devotion and a gallantry that has no precedent. We see this handful of white men controlling many many thousands of men of high courage, and occupying the position to some extent of demigod, but at any rate a leader as well as guide, philosopher, and friend. From no one does the sepoy get more disinterested and more freely given help and advice, than from his British officer, that man of alien race and a widely different faith.

Quite how or why we know not, but the fact has remained that for two centuries, with the exception of the madness of 1857, come weal come woe, come rain come shine, the sepoy has followed and trusted that unintelligible entity his sahib. From the plains of Madras to the snows of the Hindu Kush, from the Deccan to Burma, from the Punjab to China, through snow and frost and fiery furnace, the sepoy has followed the sahib, chanting the old chant of the patient East—

> *Kăbhi sŭkh aur kăbhi dŭkh*
> *Angrez ka naukar—*

which may be interpreted, "Sometimes pleasure, sometimes pain, the servant of the English."

Regular pay, due sympathy, and prompt justice may, and do, appeal to the mercenary soldier, and bring men of martial proclivities to a service in which profit and suitable recognition of devotion follow on services. But the reasonable fulfilment of the written word, the acting up to the provisions of an attestation paper, is not to account for the deeds of the Indian soldier. It was not the fulfilment of a contract that made Clive's sepoys at Arcot give up their rations to the European soldiers, or the 35th Native Infantry do the same when the earthquake killed the remaining live stock in Jellalabad. It was not the acting up to the letter of the law that kept some hundreds of Poorbeah sepoys true to their salt within the shattered defences of Lucknow, or took the Gurkha and Punjabi soldiers up and through the Delhi breaches, or made the Guides escort in Kabul sell their lives for the sake of their British officer, to the mob and the dog Heratis. No contract alone takes the native of the plains to serve the Sirkar in the snows of the Afghan hills, and to tramp the burning desert, or down to the swamps and the fever of the eastern frontier.

Some love of service, some power of the white man for attracting faithful service and admiration, must be the motive power that brings Hindu and Musalman, Afghan and Indian, Sikh and Gurkha, to an alien ruler and an alien race, to serve for small guerdon and smaller pension. For honour, no doubt, and hereditary love of the sword the man of a martial clan takes to military service; but there is more than this, and it would seem that so long as the British are worthy of it, so long as courage and justice and the strong arm keep up the confidence of a hundred races in our power to keep the ring, so long will the soldier races of the East serve the Sirkar.

The Poona Horse Standard, surmounted by a silver hand, captured at the battle of Kooshab.

It is the fashion among the unthinking to say that the bayonet of good British Atkins alone keeps us in India, and that we hold and rule India by the sword. Except, however, in a very very limited manner, and strictly subordinate sense, this is the result of a great misconception. Sir John Seeley especially pointed out the limits of this conception. He pointed out that, in the suppression of the Mutiny of the Bengal Army, the small British forces never wanted for ready assistance. Transport supplies, military followers, and domestic servants thronged to our assistance. Never for a day was the force clinging to the Ridge at Delhi in want for anything that the natives round could supply. That is to say, there was no feeling of sympathy with the rebels, or that it was disgraceful to give assistance to those opposed to the brave Indians trying to shake off an alien yoke. There was no feeling that the patriot fought for his country-side. And why ? Probably because every one knew that the sepoy could not keep the peasant and the trader in peace and safety ; nay, that he was among the first to prey on them.

Here indeed we do strike the point where the 75,000 British bayonets hold India, viz. in the confidence that they give as the strong arm, to maintain that civil power that gives safety to all races and all religions, to live their own lives against all comers. Since no other rule has done the same for over a thousand years, small wonder that the length and breadth of the country, trodden out by the companies of free-lances and the wars of the barons, welcomed those that let the old man and the maiden sleep secure o' nights. The British bayonets and that sign of might, power, and majesty and dominion that bulks so large to the Eastern mind, the "twenty yoke of the forty-pounder train," as the outward and visible sign of a strong will, *do*, in this sense, hold India. But it is not the holding of India by the sword, but rather the possession of a sword to draw against those that disturb the people. The distinction is not even a subtle one.

It was Sir John Seeley who pointed out, and any one who knows India will acknowledge it, that it is only necessary for a feeling to arise, that it is impious and disgraceful to serve the British, for the whole of our fabric to tumble like a house of cards without a shot being fired or a sword unsheathed.

Fortunately it is impossible also to imagine such a situation. For many a year, nay for many a generation, it is only the presence of the strong if alien rule that can keep religion from the throat of religion, race from race, the prince from the peasant, and the thief from the banker. Because the English can do this for a long-distracted country, with their reserve police force of 75,000 hearty English Atkinses, therefore the mass of the people serve for a wage willingly, and while serving give true and faithful service. Because also it is well to be in the train of the strong and successful, so do the martial men of India gladly serve the ruler alongside those same Atkinses.

It is no part of the scope of this book to inquire what the future may bring forth, or to peer into the crystal globe to see how long the anomaly of West nursing East to peace and prosperity and national ideals must continue, nor to discuss the pace at which the East shall share its own government with the West. To the wisest the crystal has little to tell, and we plod on trying to play the game, so that pleasure and profit may ensue to those for whom we do it. It will be enough if in the future we shall have deserved success in a problem as large and as difficult as ever faced the Empire of Rome.

The strategical aspect of the great army in India also is far removed from this, the outline history of how the great army has grown and come to its present stage. But since armies in modern times do not exist for the pleasure and pomp of kings, but to some stern purpose, the extraordinarily favourable position of India and the Indian Army for the purposes of empire may be alluded to. Amphibious war, war by land and by sea, has for many years been a peculiar asset of the British Empire. The power of transporting troops to distant scenes, and to protect them on the high seas, has belonged to Britain. Since ships do not sail over dry land, it is not the omnipotent navy alone that can clinch a war. The peculiar power that we have possessed in the past, to land our troops at that point where their very presence must produce an effect far out of proportion to

Havildar,
Marine Battalion, 1885.

their actual numbers, is one of those that only the mistress of the seas can hope to wield. This power and all it stands for is aptly described by Captain Mahan, when talking of the influence of sea-power, and the small red ulcer that it enabled us to keep open in Spain. He writes of the "Storm-beaten ships, on which the Grand Army never looked, that stood between it and the dominion of the world."

These same storm-beaten ships equally protected expeditions overseas from India. From India as from a fresh base we are able to send forth expeditions at the bidding of an ocean cable which other powers can but start from Europe. Time after time has India sent her native army over the sea on Imperial quests in return for the peace we give her. Manila, Macao, Java, Bourbon, Egypt in 1801, Egypt in modern times, China time after time, have seen the native troops from India bearing their share of an Imperial purpose. The army of India exists for its own protection and security, but, in return for the British backing that forms its nucleus, is ready, when its own immediate needs are not pressing, to contribute to the general purpose of empire. The sepoy has carried the Eagles in triumph from the shores of the Mediterranean to the Great Wall of China, and to those who see fit to inquire how long he will continue to do so, the answer is perfectly straightforward. Just so long as our rule in India fulfils the conditions that have hitherto made it acceptable to a people longing for peace and protection.

A Russian officer who has lately given to the world his impressions of a tour in India, in paying tribute to the faithful soldiery and their military bearing and efficiency, has exactly described the situation. He is mindful that the Indian soldier has for centuries served the ruler, and remarks that he, like the cat, is attached to the house rather than to the master.

For at present

Khălk-i-Khuda
Mulk-i-Sirkar
Hukm-i-Sahiban Alishan.[1]

---

[1] Mankind belongs to God,
The land to the Government,
And power to the powerful Sahibs.

THE END